# Biggest Little Photographer

Photography
By Thomas Darnell

With help from
Camilla Downs

Loving Kindness Books

First Printing October 2016



Cover design by LeRue Press, LLC

Printed in the United States of America

LCCN 2016953428

ISBN 978-0-9800568-2-2


Photography by Thomas Darnell
Content and Layout by Camilla Downs

To all those who knew they could get something done, and did.
*- Thomas Darnell*

Life is what happens between being inspired to do something and the day you finish doing that something. Don't miss out on life by never starting or being consumed by the finishing. Here's to all who live from the heart and share that with others. May you never lose your childlike sense of wonder.
*- Camilla Downs*

Author's Note:

This is not simply a photography book and not a photography book by a professional photographer. This book is about an 8 year old boy, with a passion for LEGO, and a huge heart.

This is a book with a message that life *is what happens from here to there, what happens between deciding what you want and receiving that which you want.*

It's a book about an 8 year old boy who read an article about a professional photographer who had taken photographs of a minifigure taking photographs for 365 days. An 8 year old boy who then asked, "Can I do that?" When he was told, "Yes, you can", he then bought a minifigure camera with his own money.

An 8 year old boy who used what he had, a donated iPhone 3Gs, minifigure pieces already owned, and spent less than $2.00 to purchase the camera piece.

So, while you won't find photographs of the highest quality and clarity within this book, you will find love, wonder, inspiration, and the knowing that whatever you dream, whatever you want to accomplish, it CAN be done.

And you will find that life is what happens between asking, "Can I do that?" and "I DID IT!"

It's about an 8 year old boy who, with determination and fun, completed a ONE YEAR photography project from the time he was 8 years old and ending at 9 years old.

Camilla Downs,

Mom to Thomas Darnell

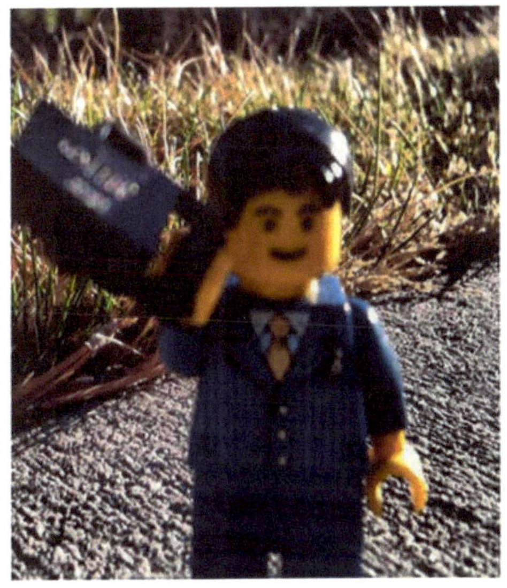

Hey friends! I'm Mr. Minifigure Photographer, also known as The Biggest Little Photographer. One day in March 2014, 8 year old Thomas Darnell, was inspired by an article his mom shared with him. He bought me a minifigure size camera and I travelled with him everywhere he went for 365 days straight.

Thomas and his mom and sister, Lillian, are nature lovers so I took lots of pictures of trees, clouds, the sky, and landscapes. I also took pictures of Thomas' simple everyday life and pictures of wherever his mom happened to be running errands that day.

I even got to ride on a horse, the beautiful Meg! And guess what? I got to travel on an airplane all the way to Stamford, Connecticut to attend the 2014 Chromosome 18 Registry & Research Society Family Conference.

We had a couple of bloopers along the way too. I went with Thomas to a summer camp with the Great Basin Naturalists. He took a disposable camera with him to take pictures because they didn't want anyone to bring phones. You will not believe this! After camp, Thomas and his family moved and they lost the disposable camera!

The other blooper is that I got lost for a couple of months. I tried and tried to help Thomas and his family find me, but they couldn't hear or see me. I was in a small pocket in a backpack Thomas had used when going for a hike with his grandpa.

Get ready for a seek and find! If you look closely you will see the "replacement" Thomas used while I was lost. He has a different style of hair, and, get ready for this …. A frying pan as the camera! Thomas' mom, Camilla, is a ninja improvisor and she helped him with finding a replacement until I was found. Whew!

Thomas posted the pictures daily on his instagram account and purposely never showed my face until the very last day! I sure hope you enjoy the pictures I took and it is my deepest wish that you are inspired by my and Thomas' year long adventure.

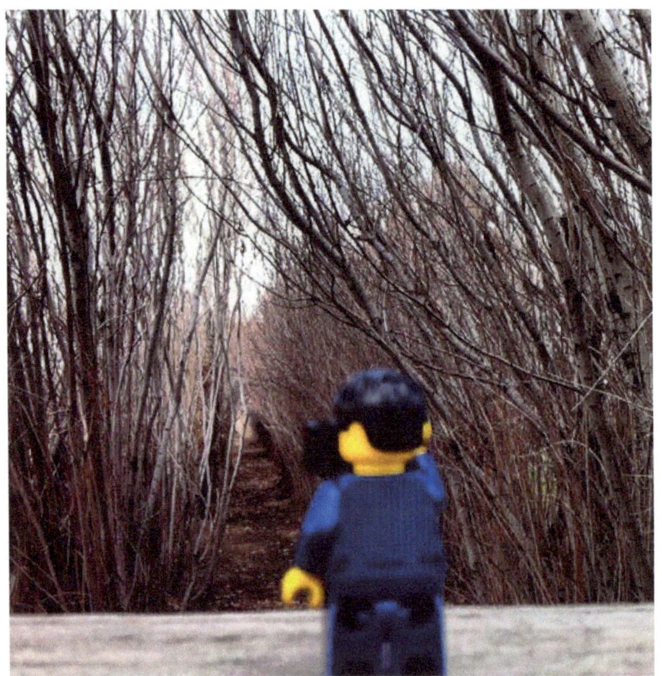

"And, when you want something, all the universe conspires in helping you to achieve it."

— *Paulo Coelho*

# LANDMARKS

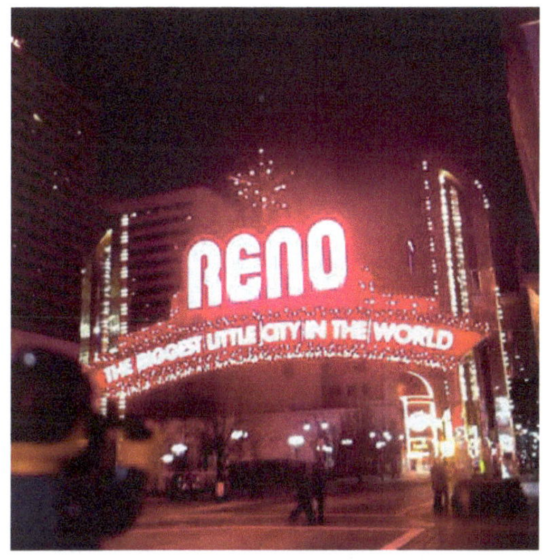


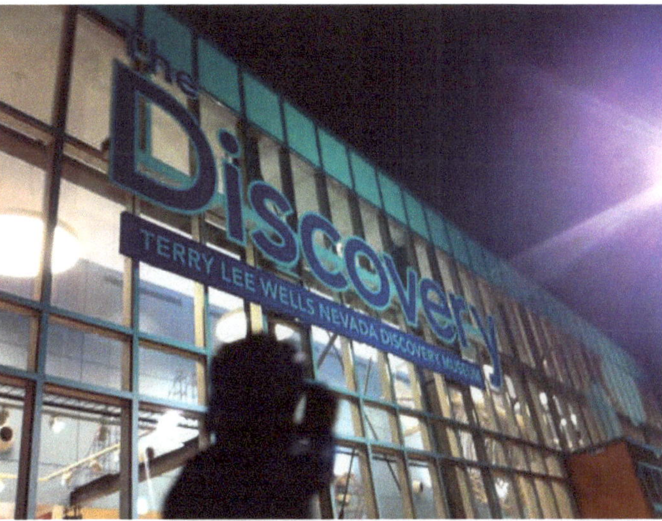


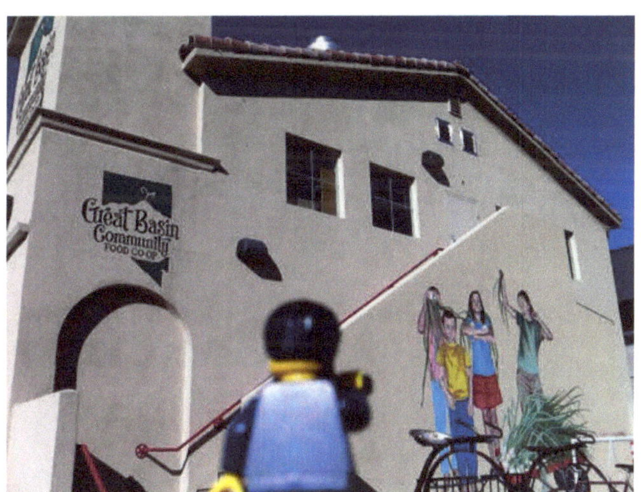


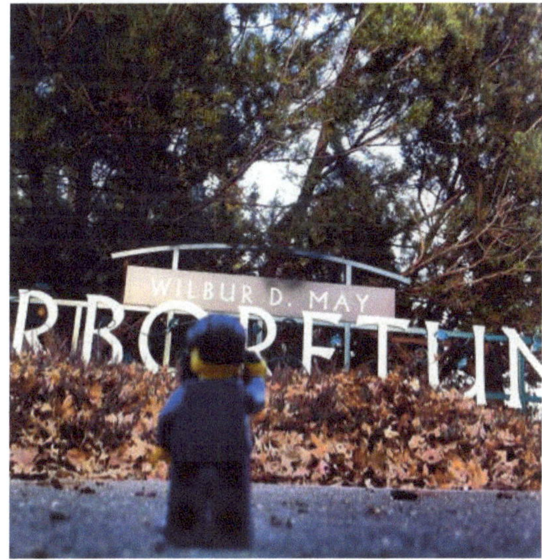


"Life is either a great adventure or nothing."
— Helen Keller

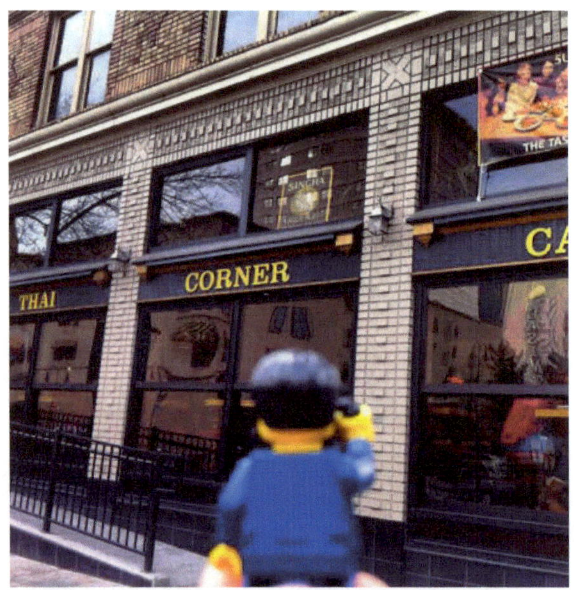

THAI CORNER
CA


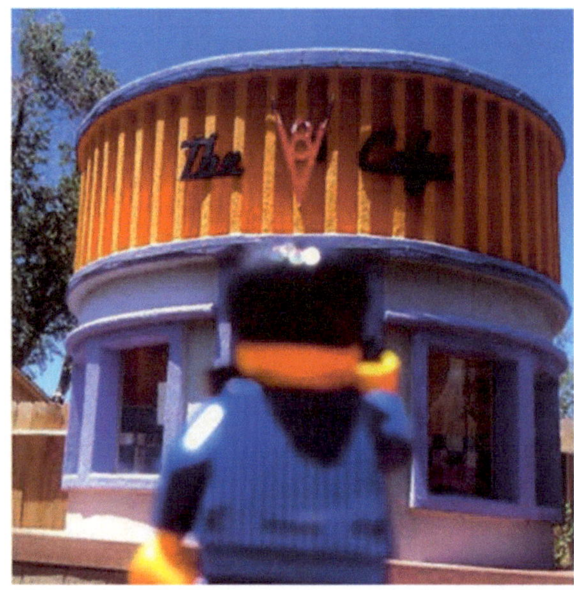

The C


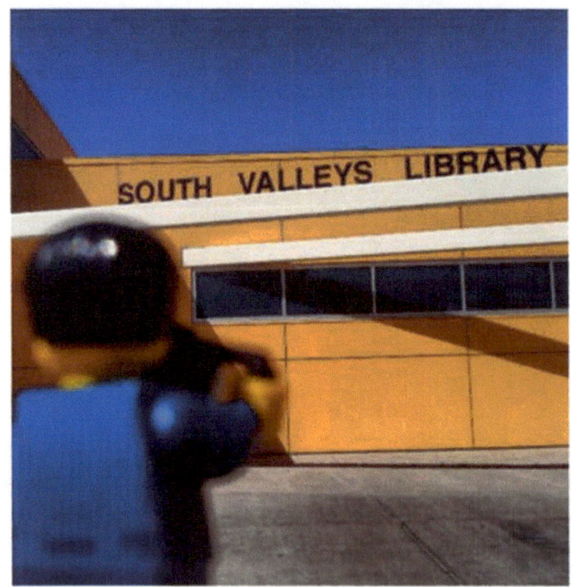

SOUTH VALLEYS LIBRARY


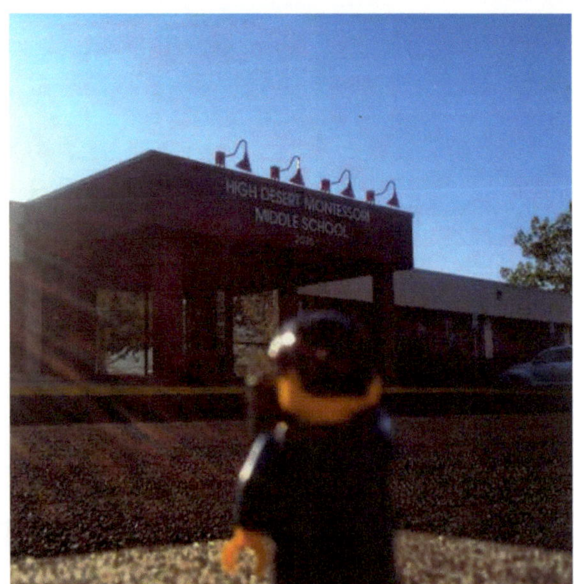

HIGH DESERT MONTESSORI
MIDDLE SCHOOL

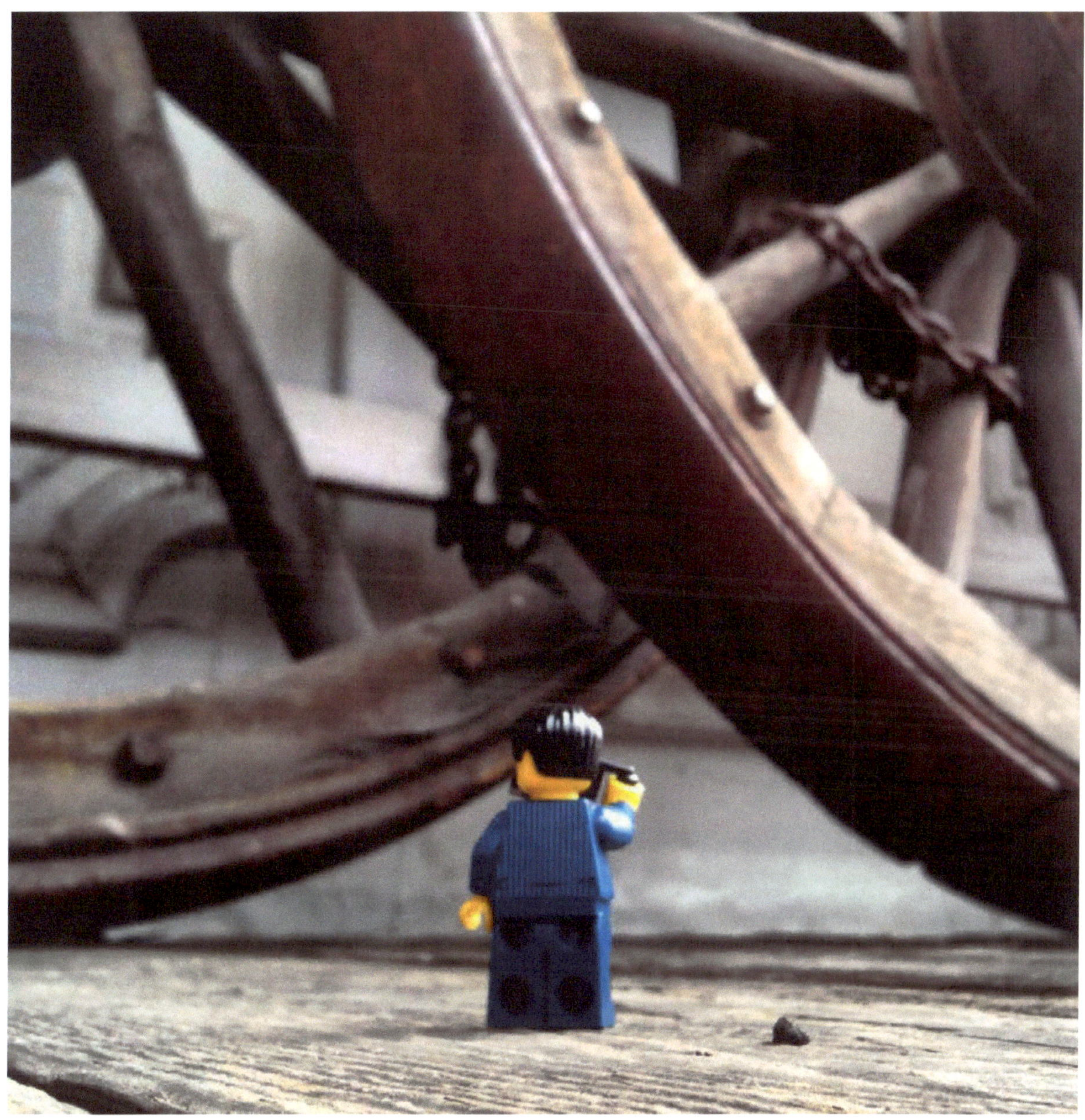

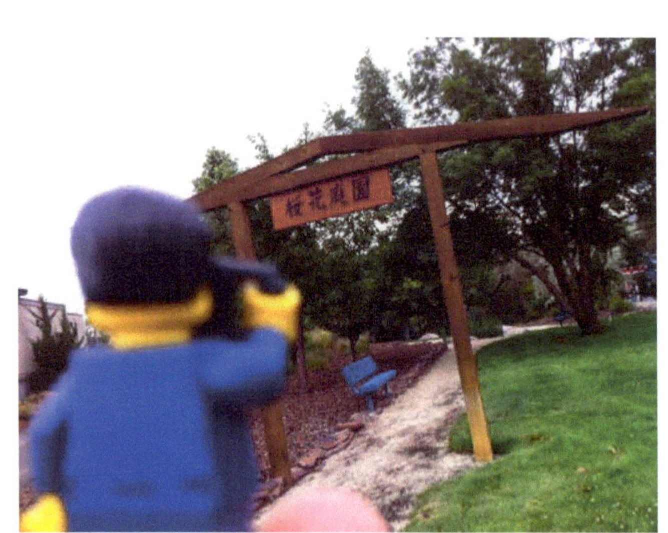

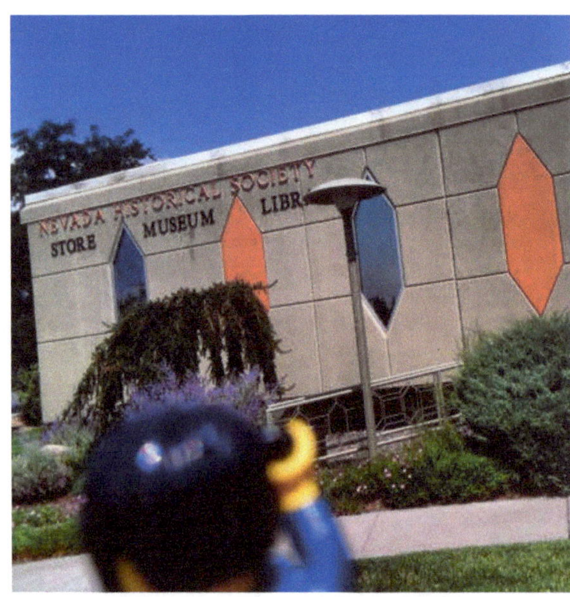

NEVADA HISTORICAL SOCIETY
STORE    MUSEUM    LIBR


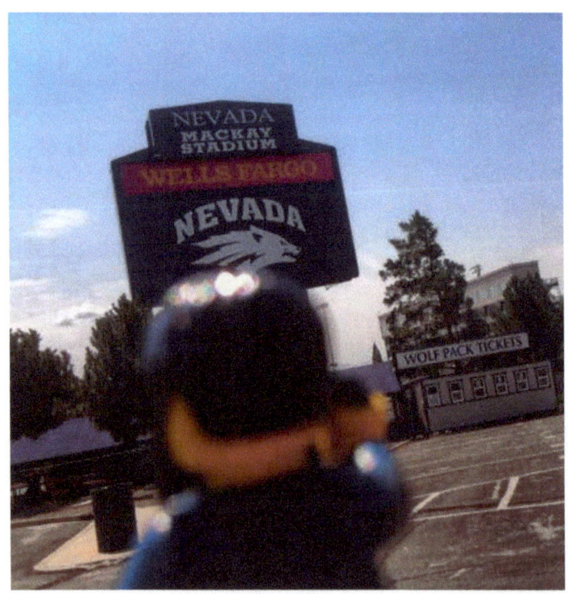

NEVADA
MACKAY
STADIUM
WELLS FARGO
NEVADA
WOLF PACK TICKETS


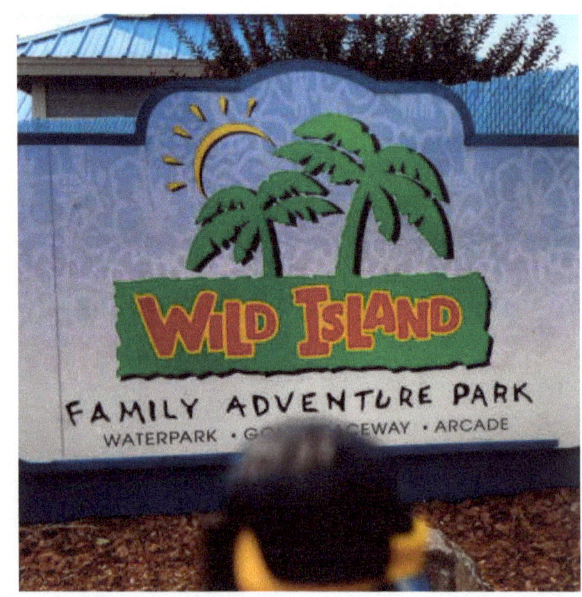

WILD ISLAND
FAMILY ADVENTURE PARK
WATERPARK • GO-KART RACEWAY • ARCADE

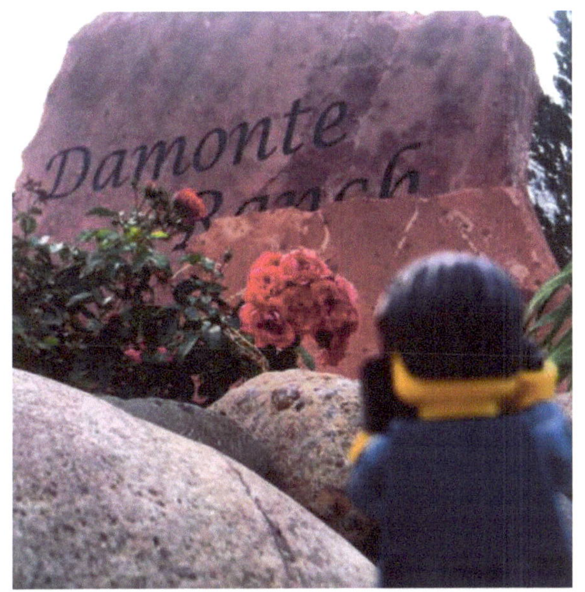
Damonte
Ranch

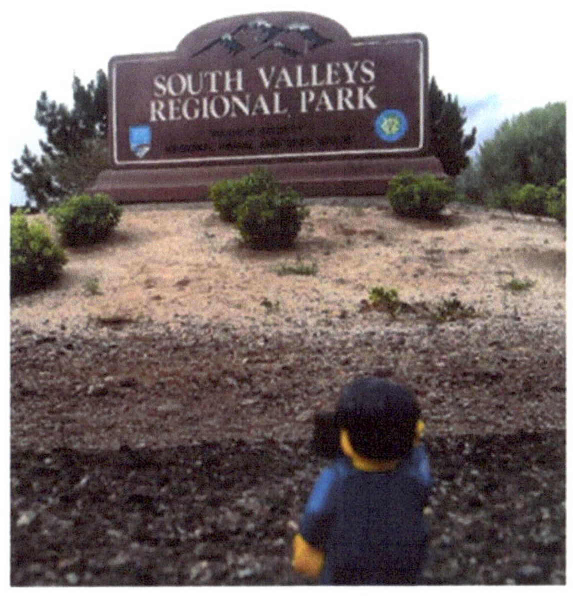
SOUTH VALLEYS
REGIONAL PARK

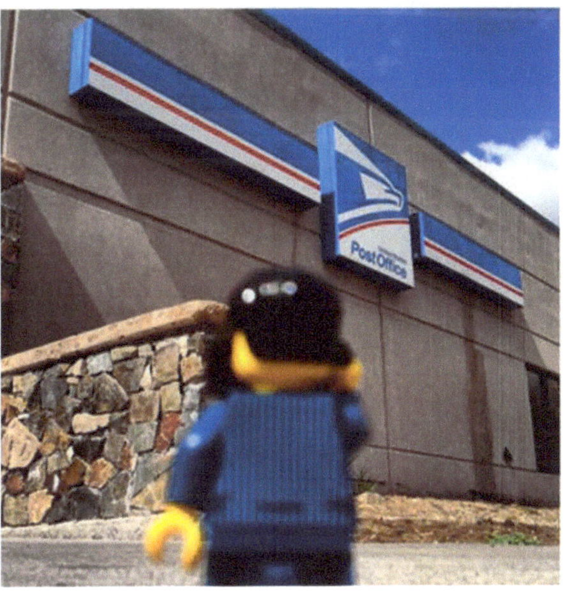
Post Office

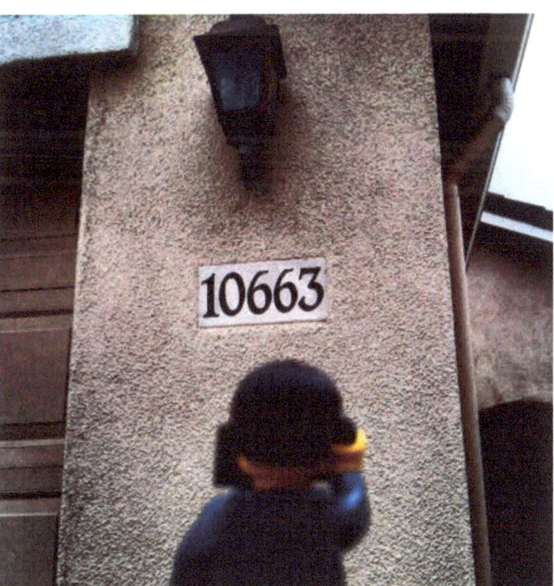
10663

*Thomas Darnell*

# OUT AND ABOUT AND AROUND THE HOUSE

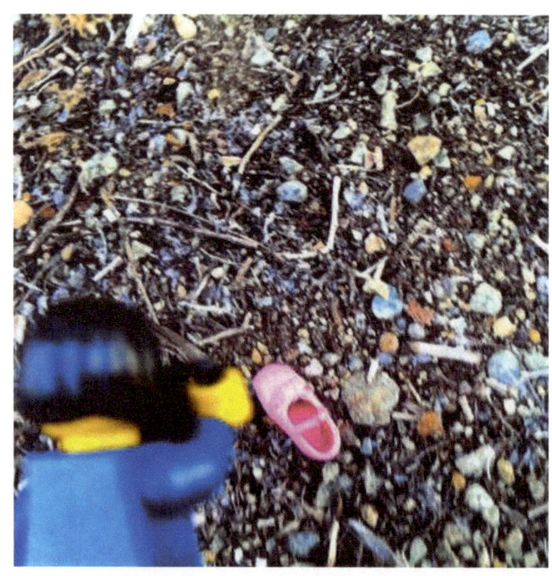

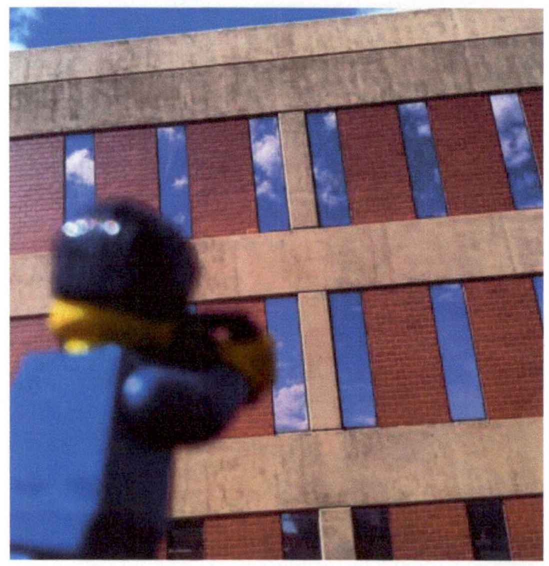

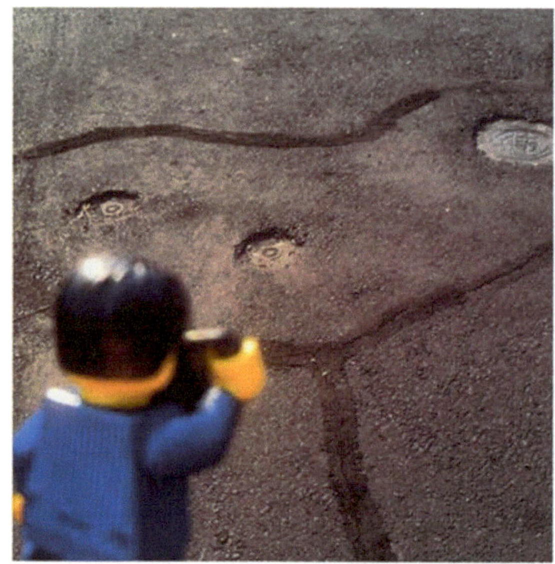

"I find television very educating. Every time somebody turns on the set, I go into the other room and read a book."

— *Groucho Marx*

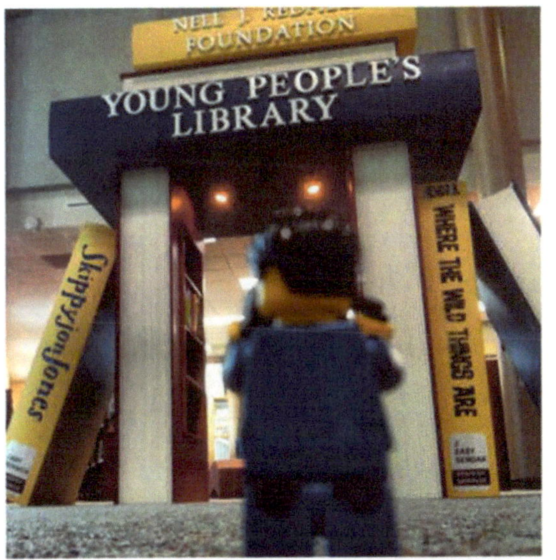

NELL J. REDF...
FOUNDATION
YOUNG PEOPLE'S
LIBRARY
Skippyjon Jones
WHERE THE WILD THINGS ARE


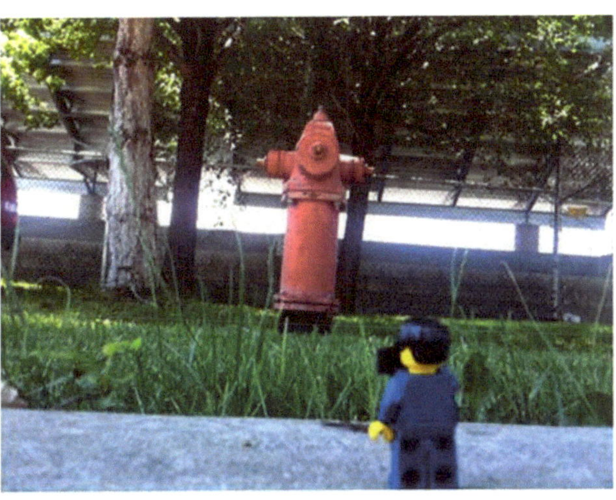

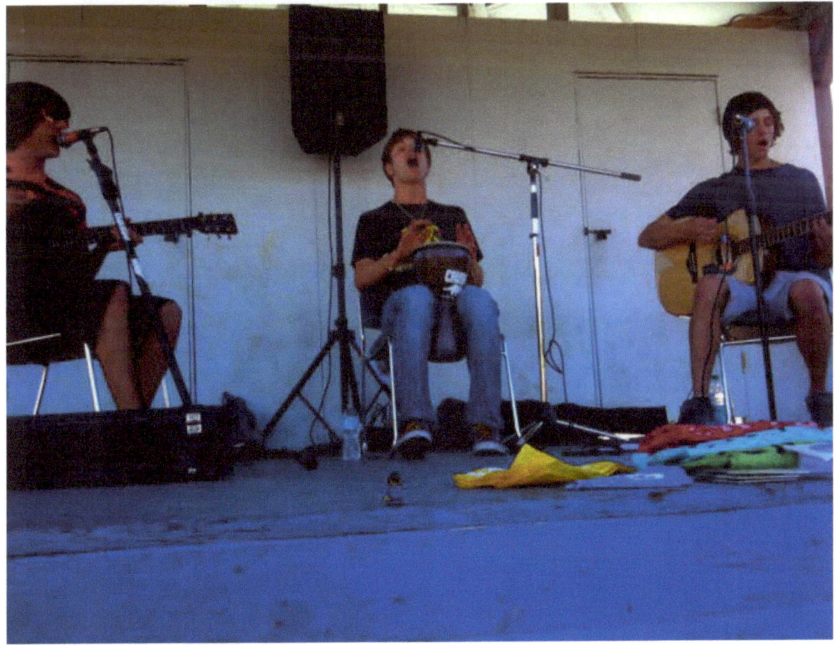

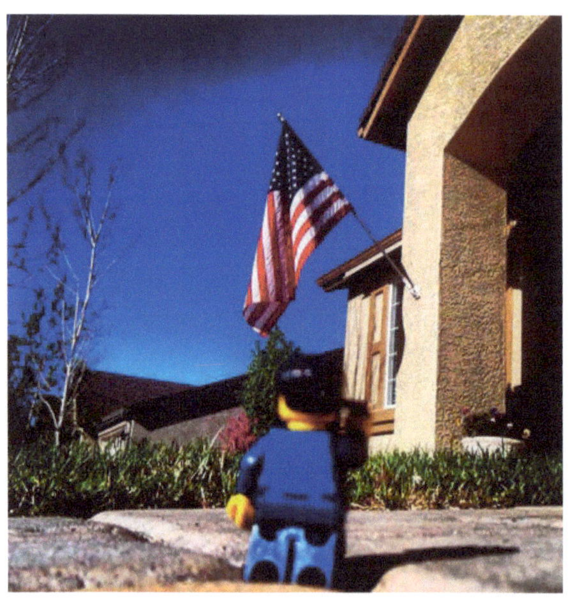

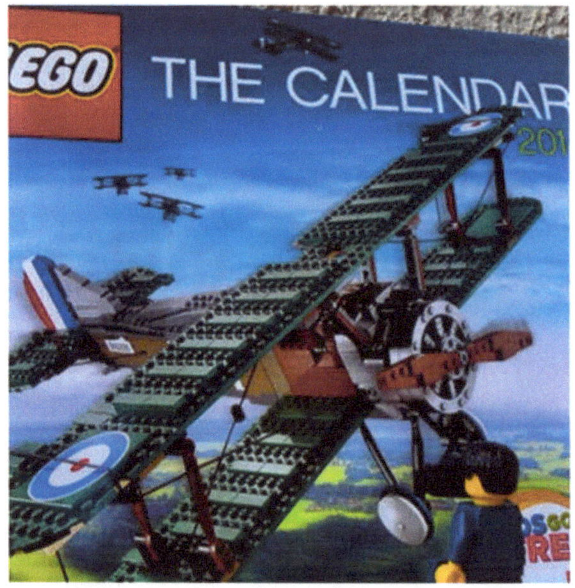
EGO
THE CALENDAR
201

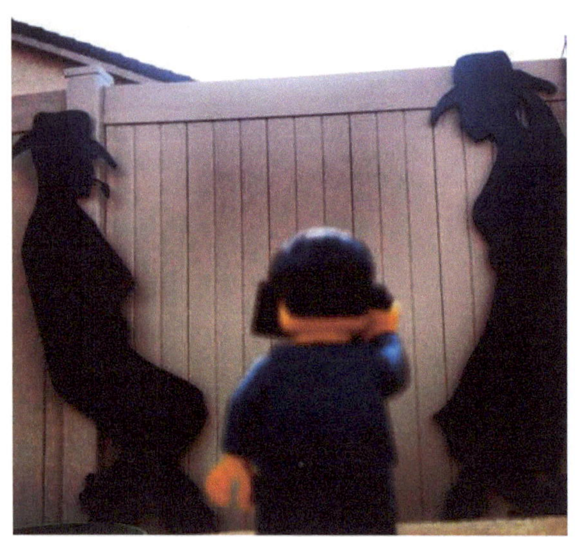

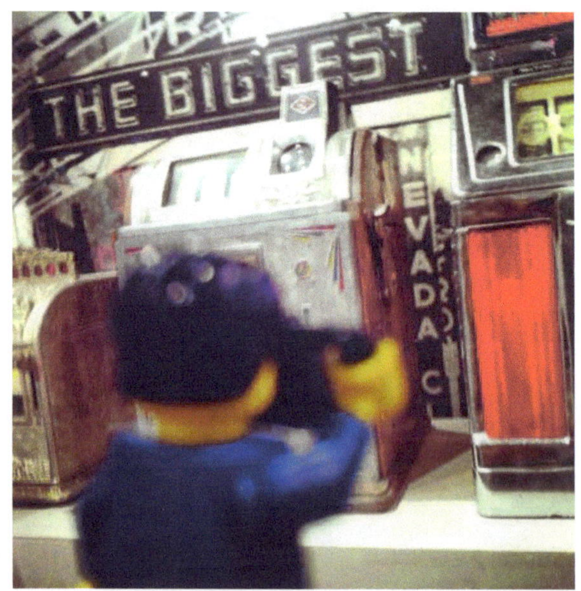
THE BIGGEST
NEVADA

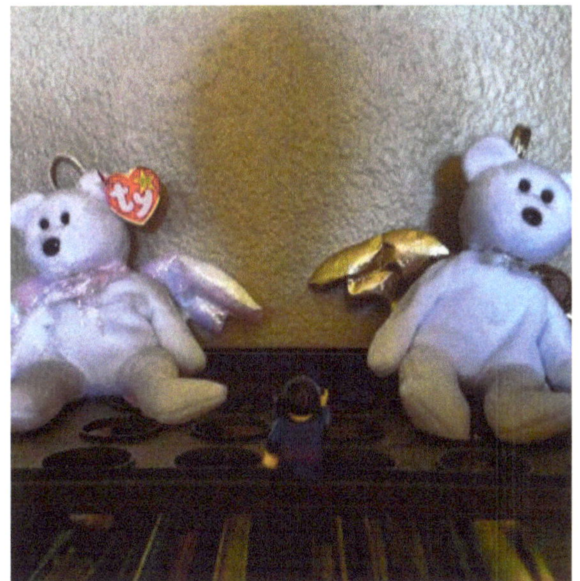

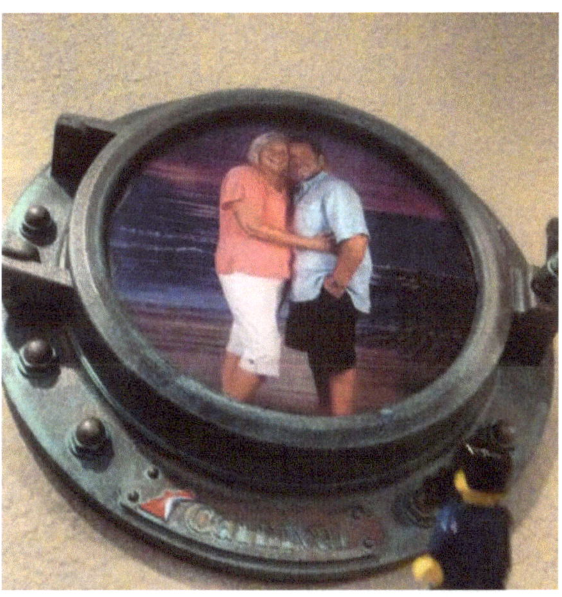

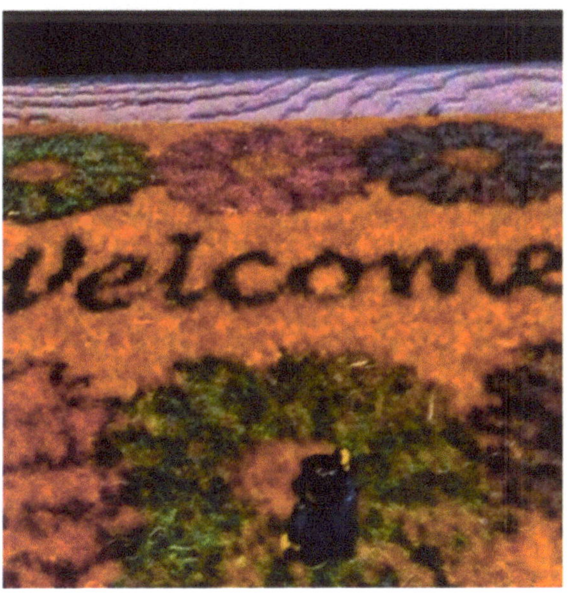

welcome


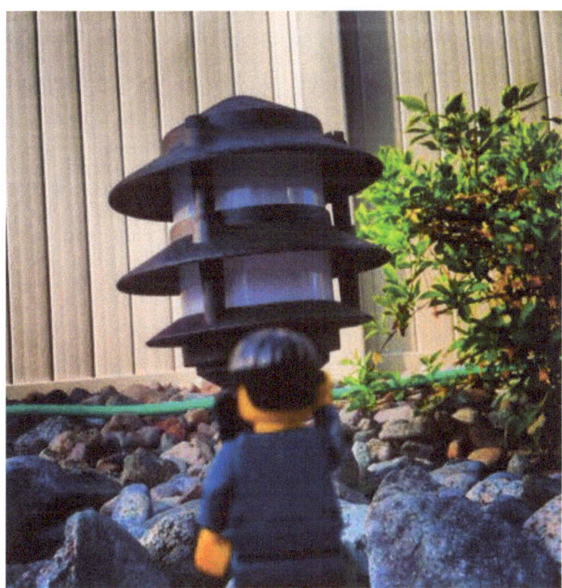

Thomas Darnell

# THE BEAUTY OF NATURE

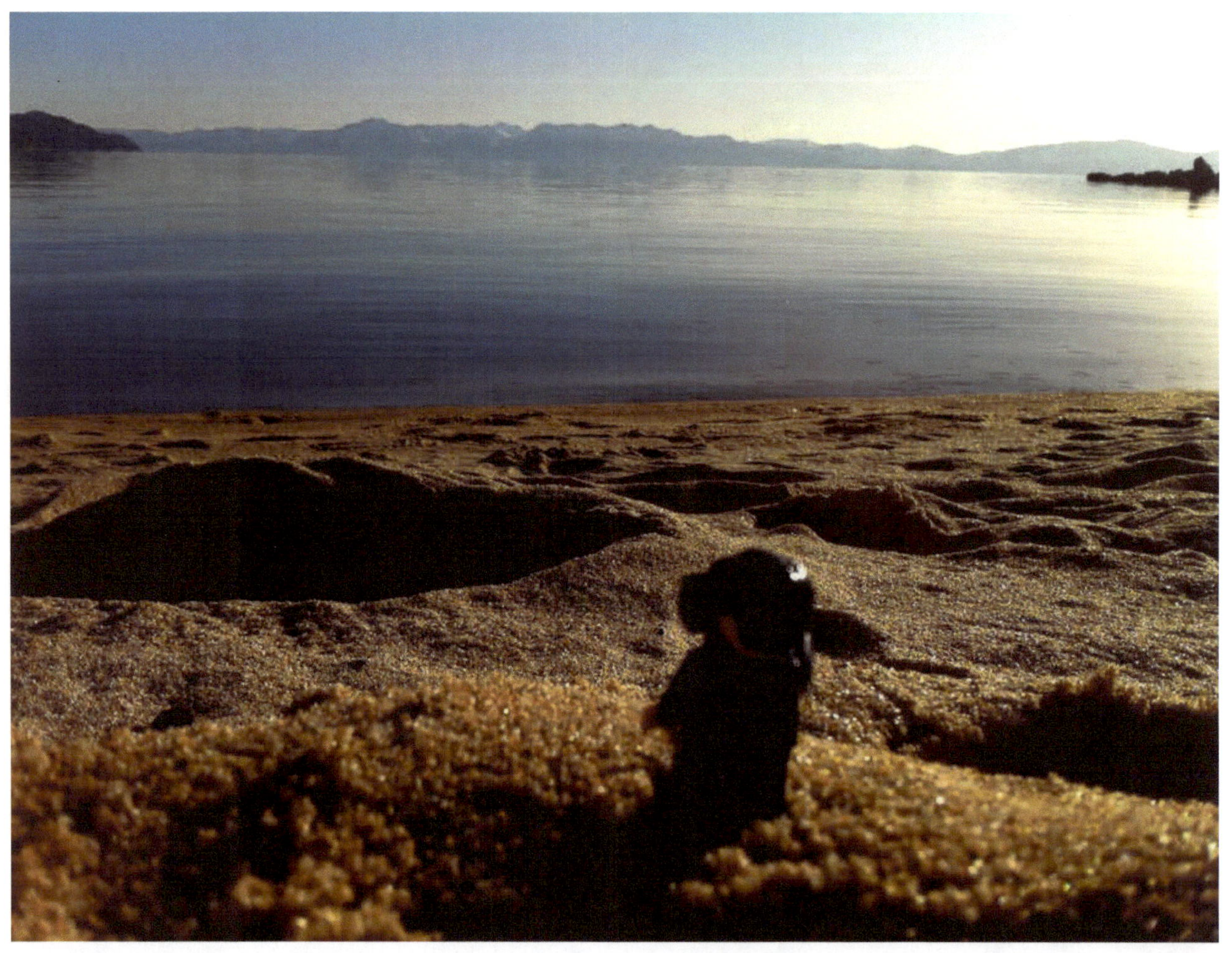

"Go to Nature's School - the one true university."
— John Muir

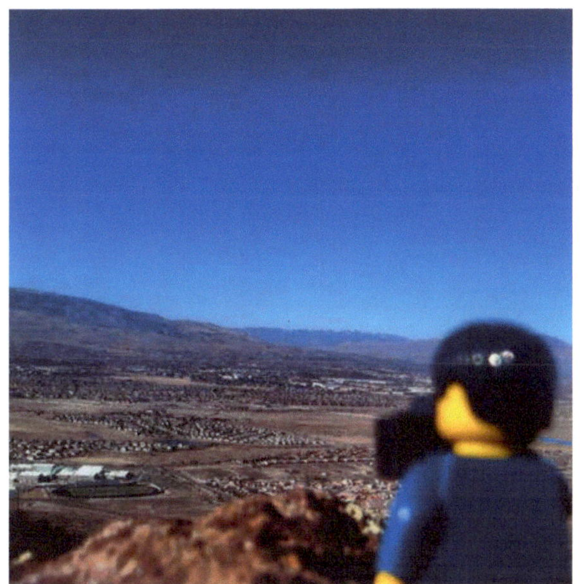
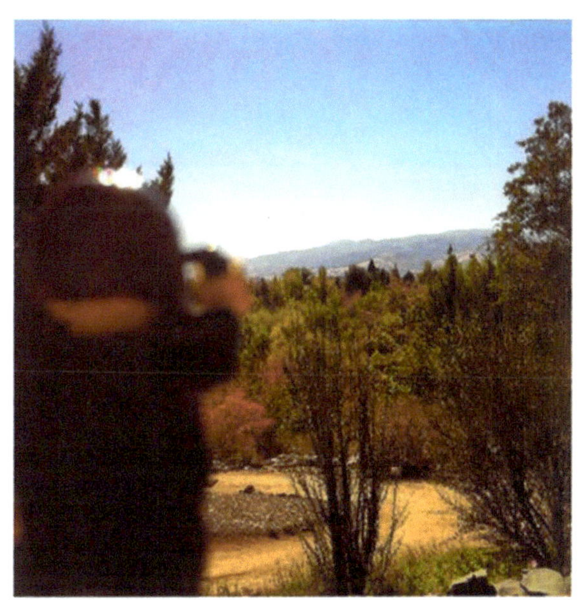
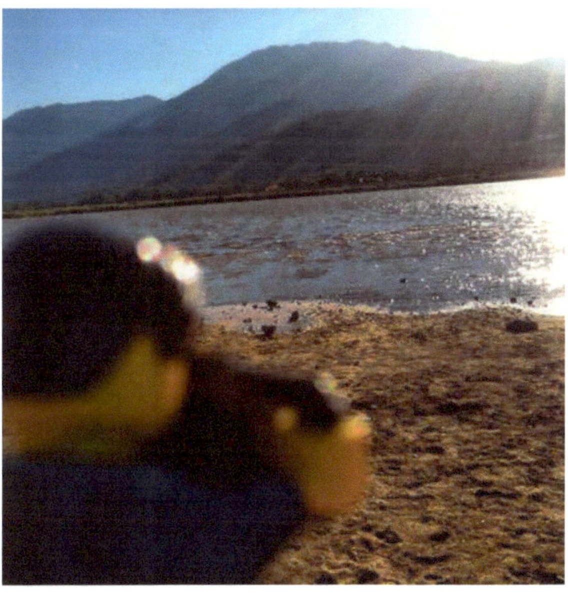
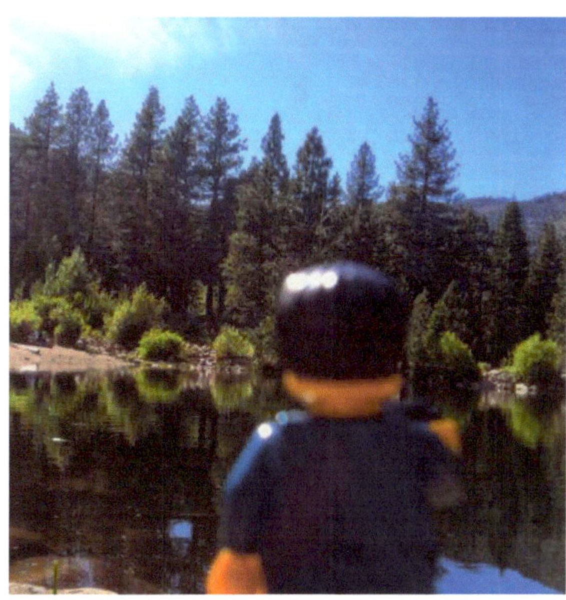

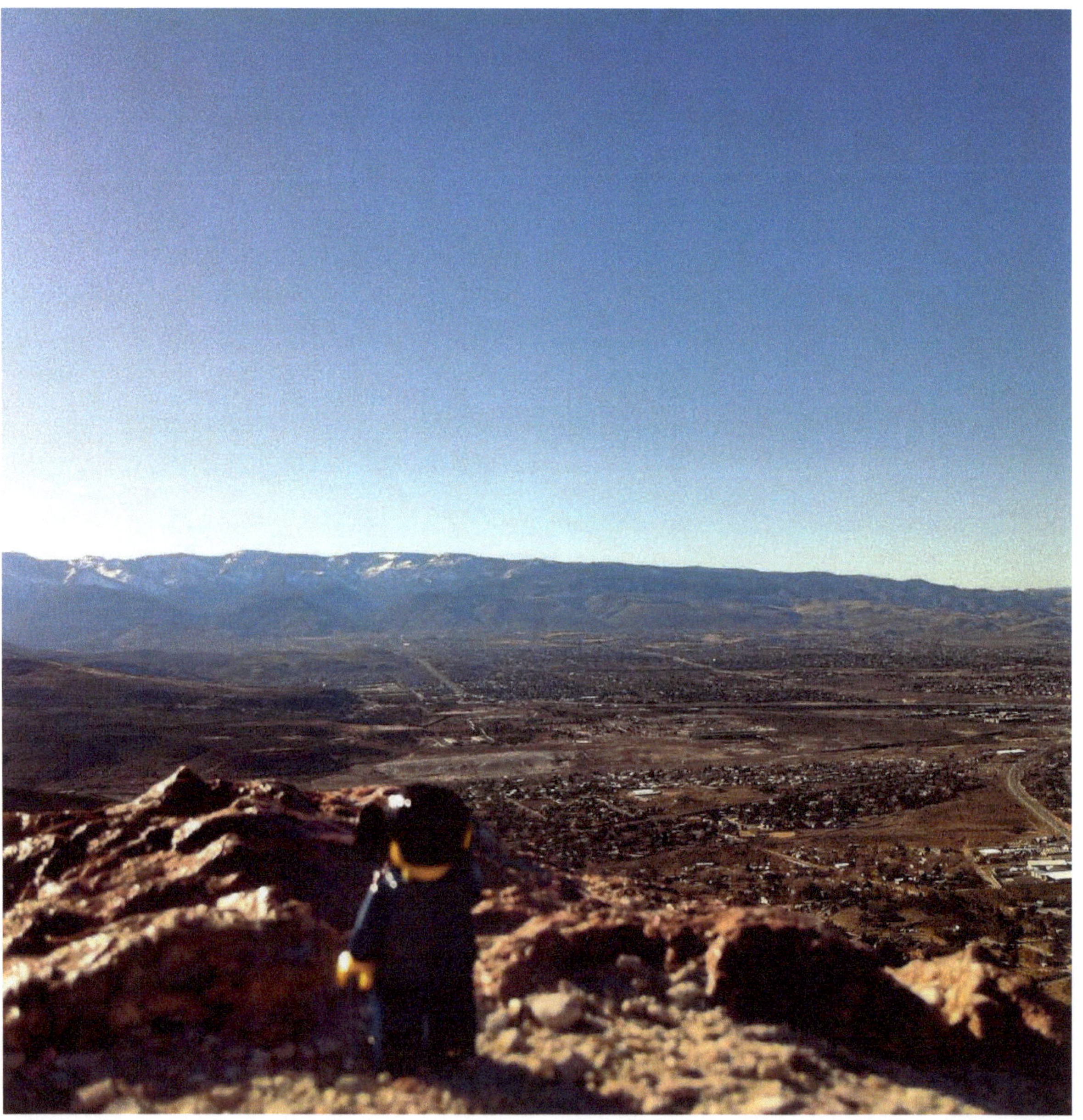

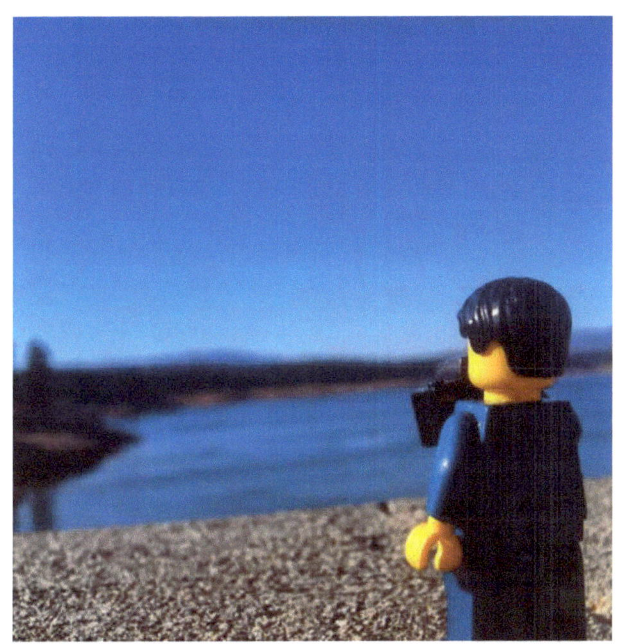

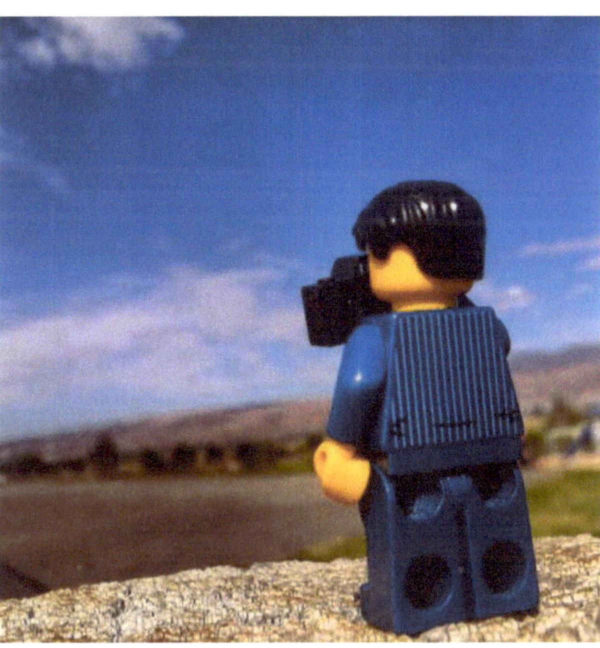

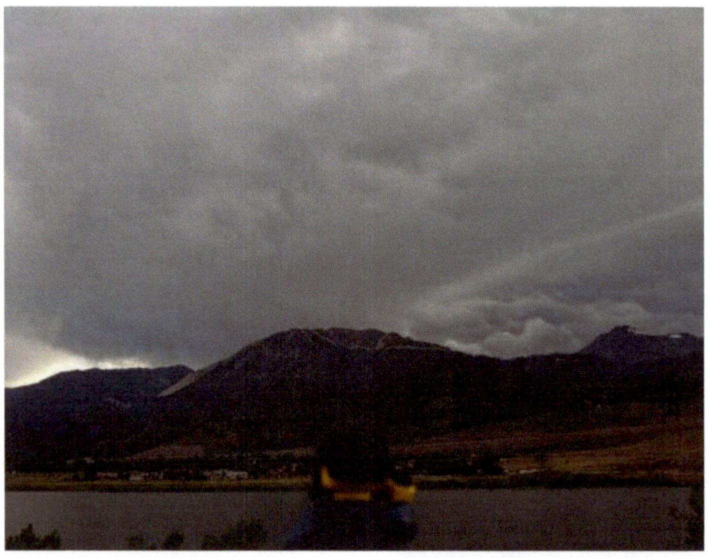

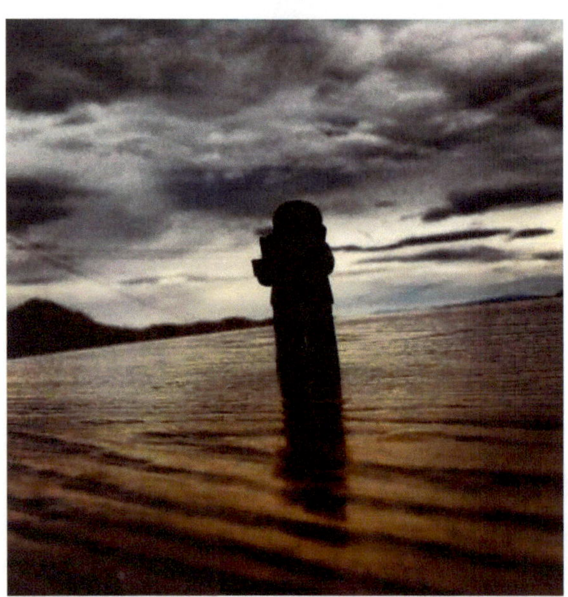

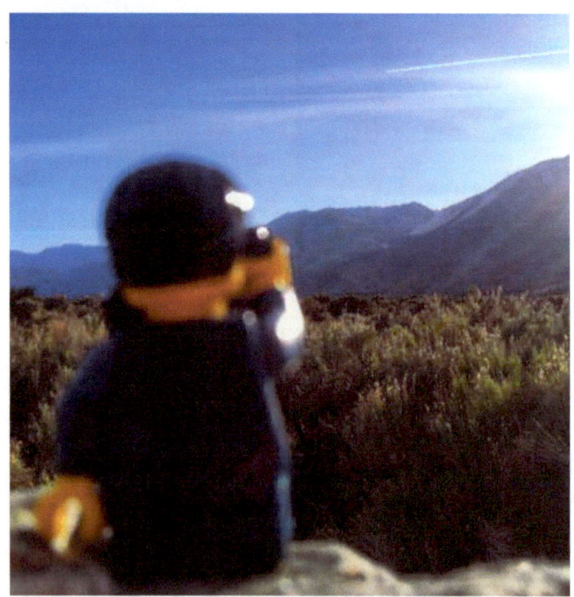

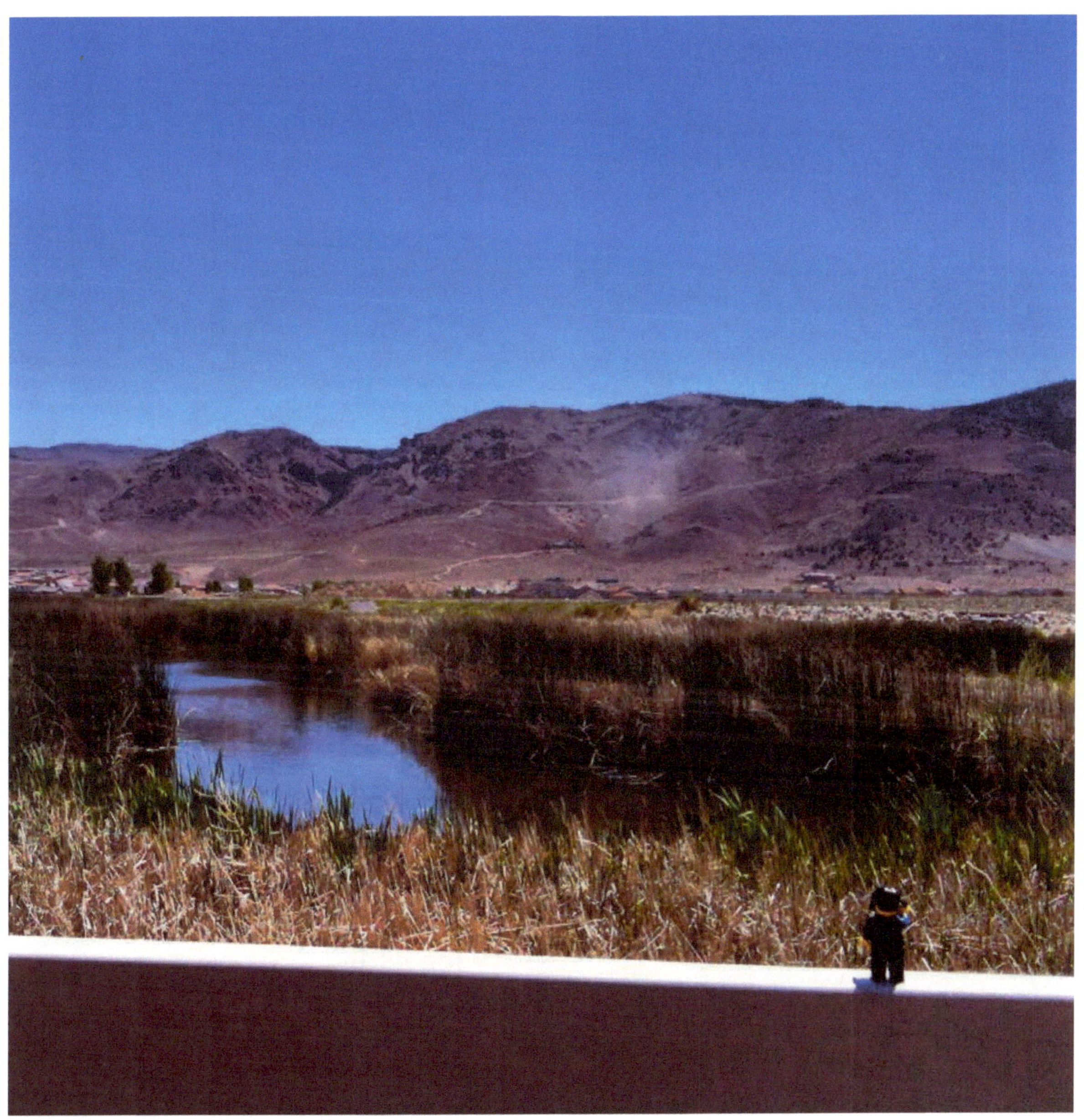

# NEWS, INFORMATION, AND COMMUNICATION

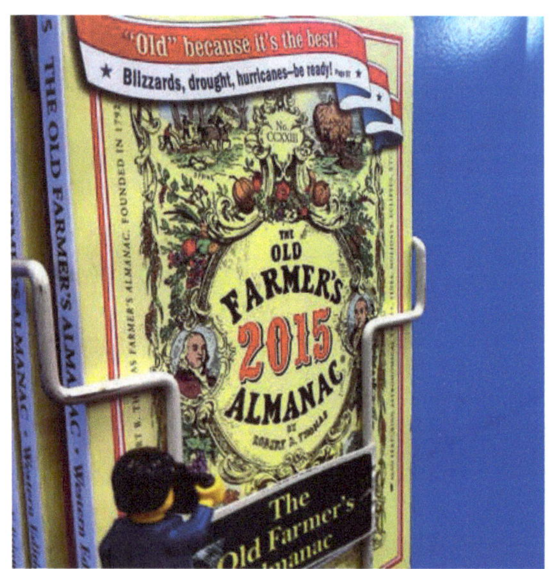

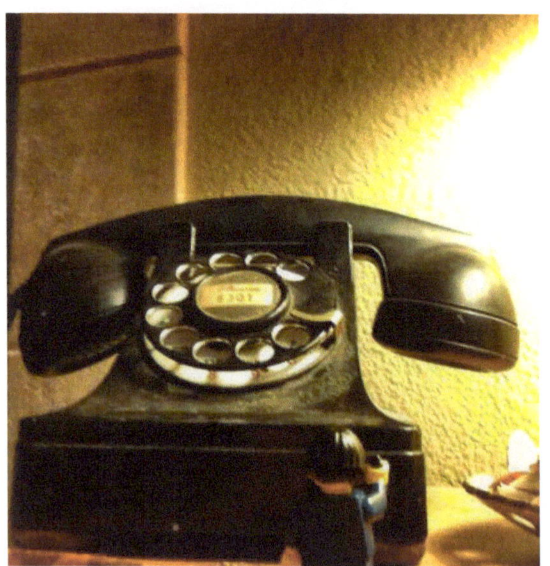

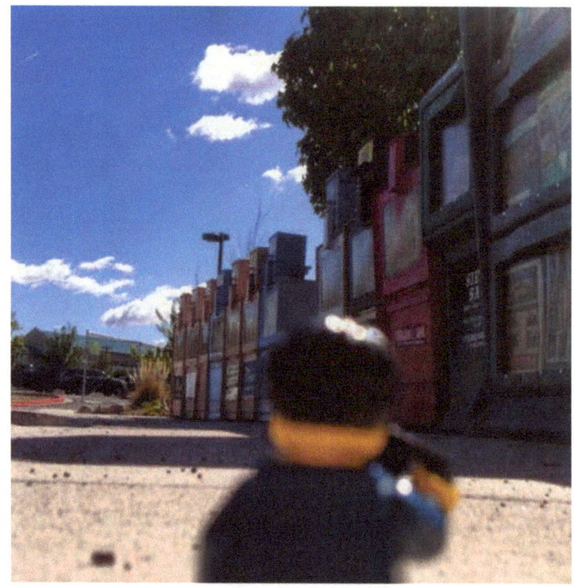

"We have two ears and one mouth so that we can listen twice as much as we speak."
-Epicetus

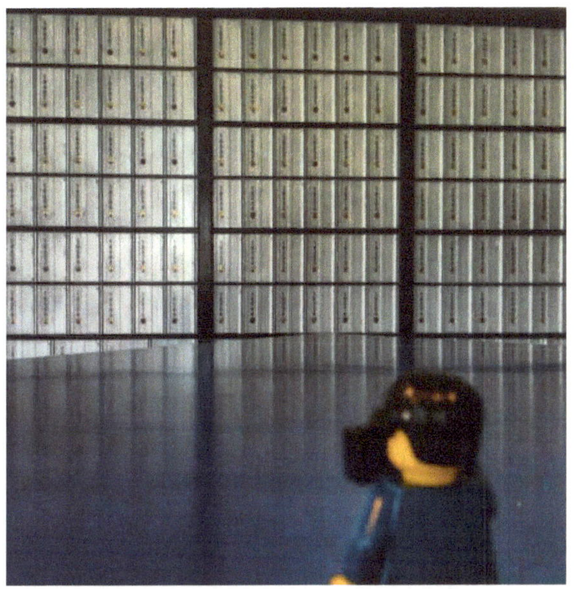

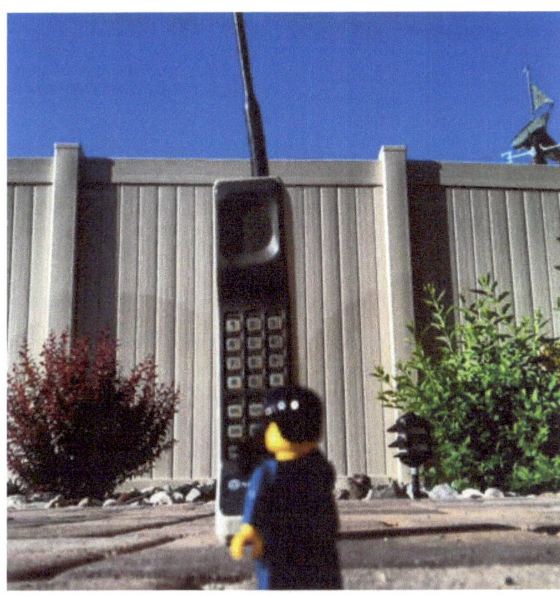

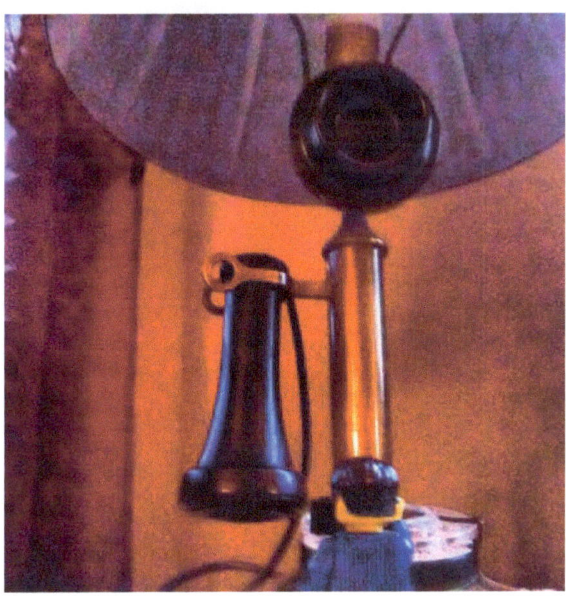

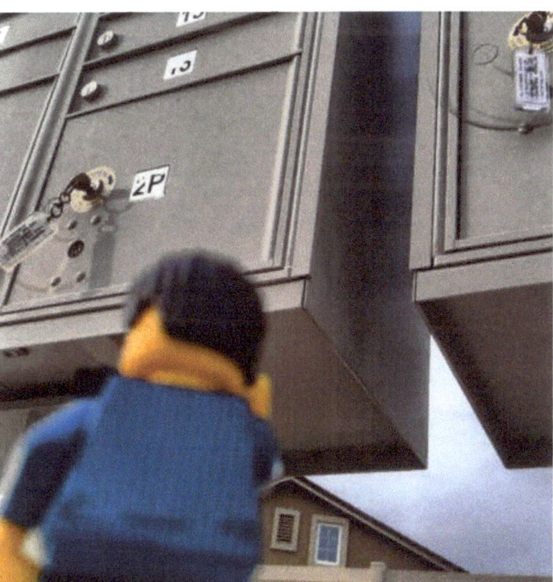

Thomas Darnell

# VEHICLES, EQUIPMENT, AND TRANSPORTATION

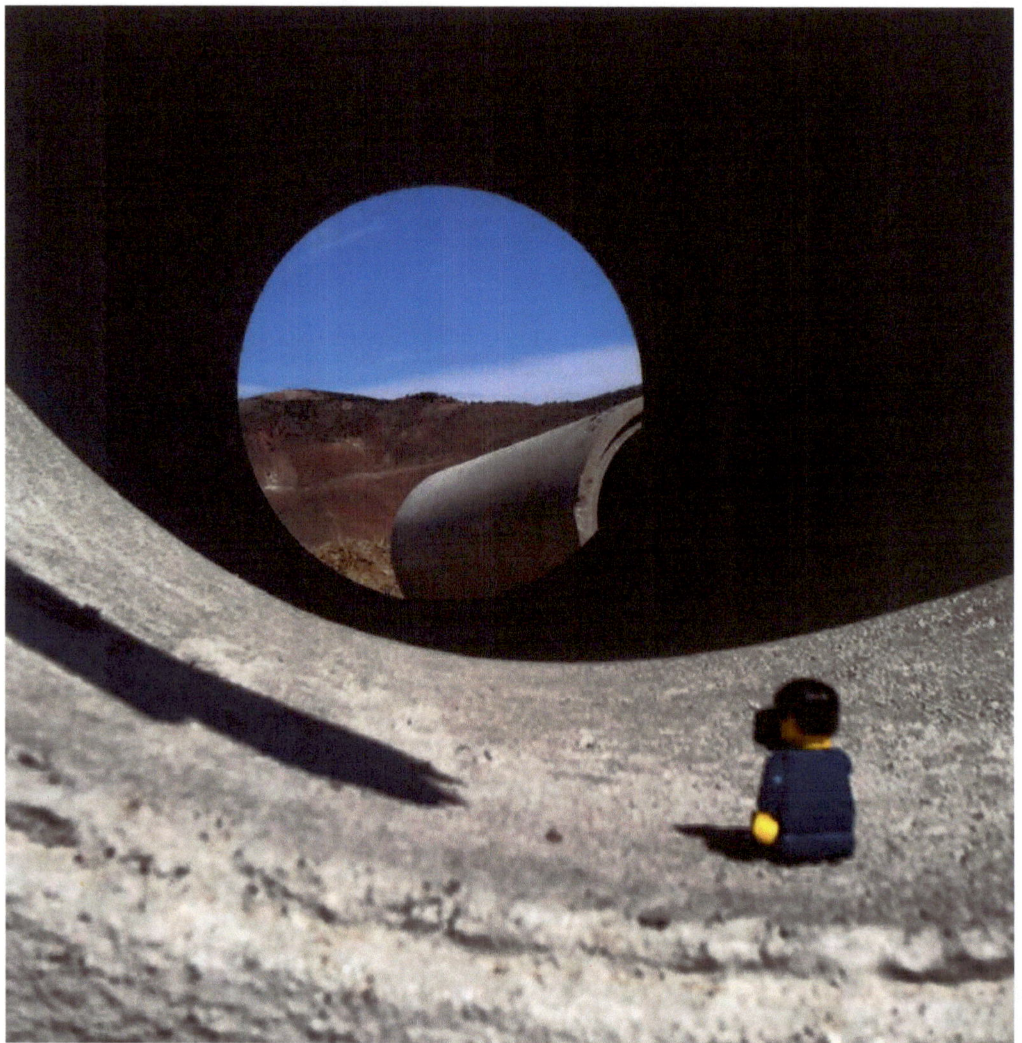

"Life is like riding a bicycle. To keep your balance, you must keep moving."
— Albert Einstein

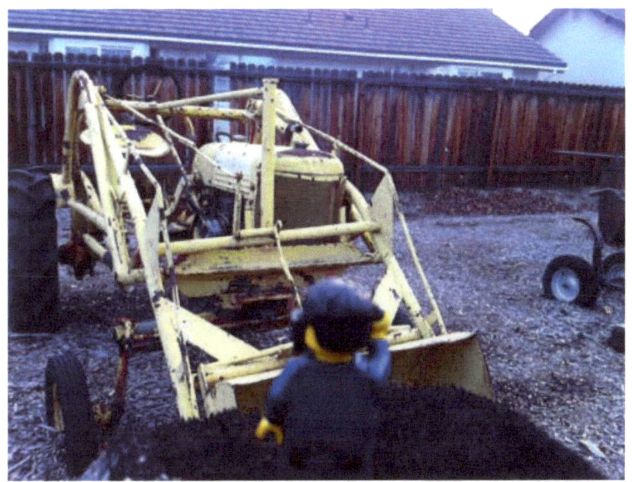

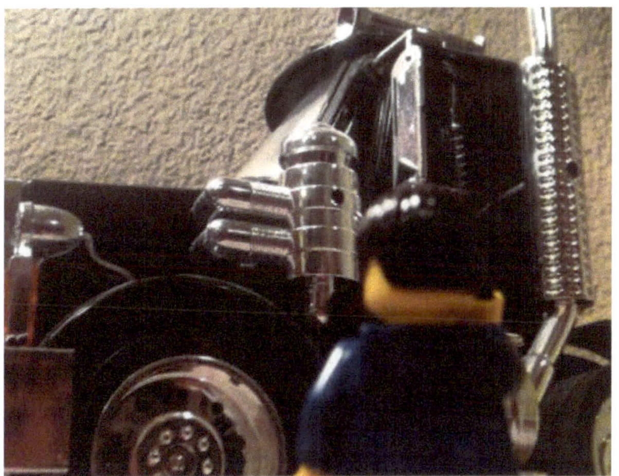

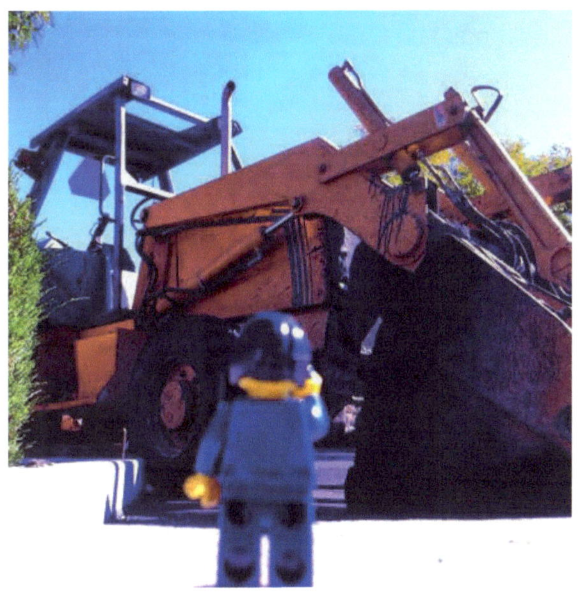

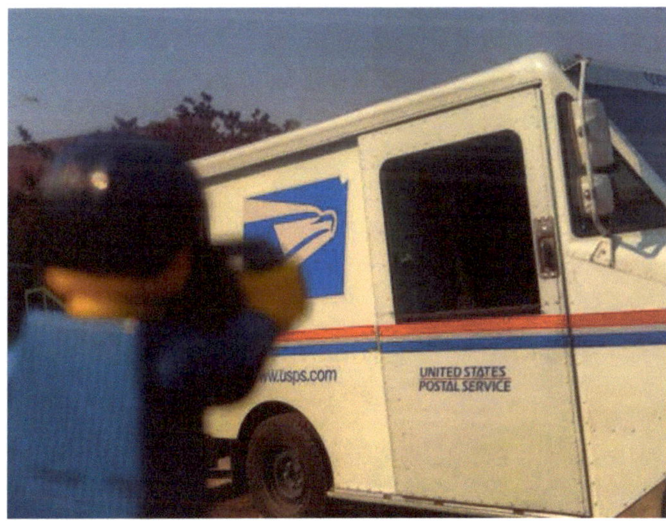

www.usps.com
UNITED STATES
POSTAL SERVICE

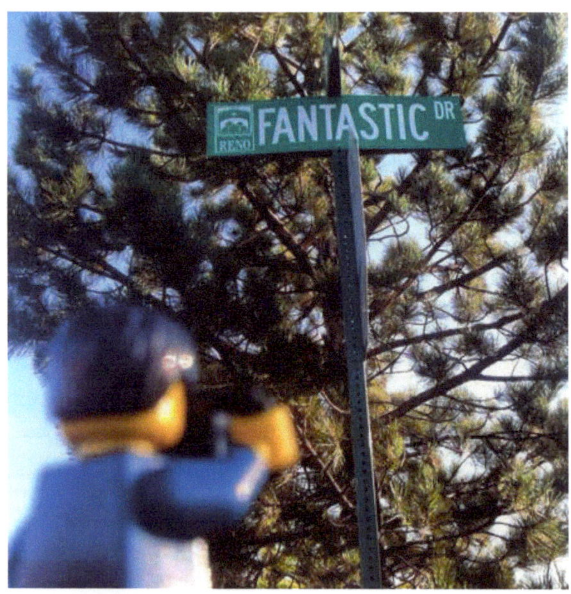
RENO
FANTASTIC DR

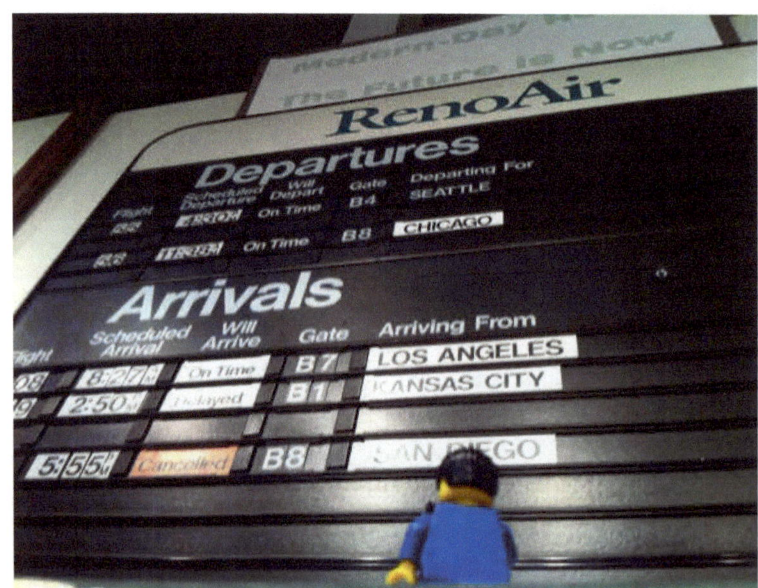
Modern-Day
the Future is Now
RenoAir
Departures
Scheduled   Will      Gate   Departing For
Departure   Depart
Flight                   B4     SEATTLE
            On Time
            On Time    B8     CHICAGO

Arrivals
Scheduled   Will      Gate   Arriving From
Arrival     Arrive
Flight
            8:27      On Time   B7   LOS ANGELES
            2:50      Delayed   B1   KANSAS CITY
            5:55      Cancelled B8   SAN DIEGO

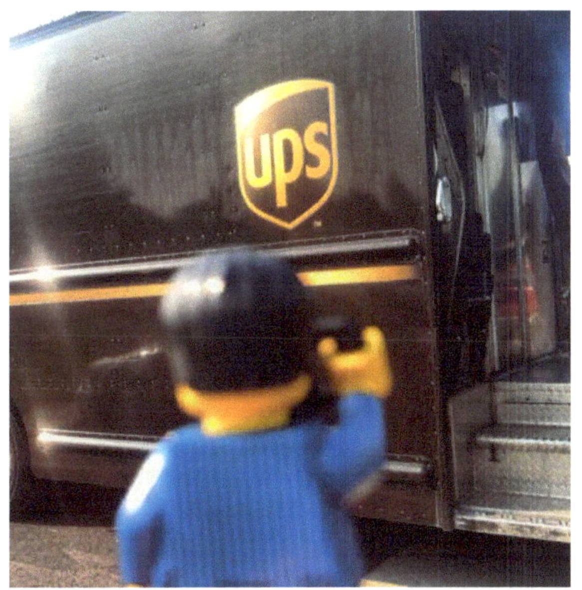

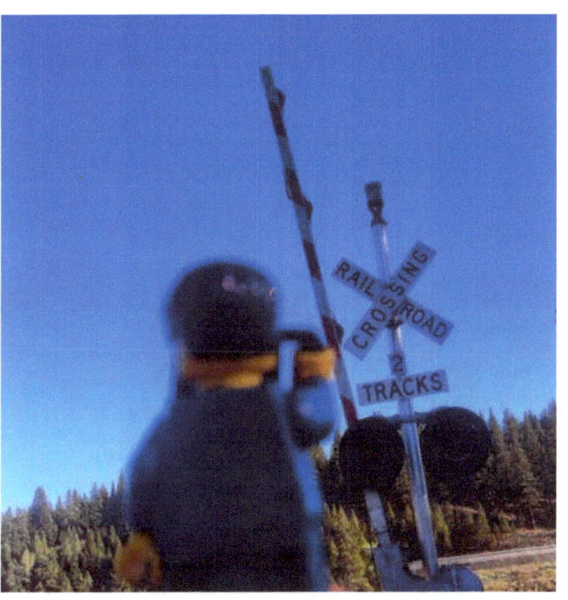


RAILROAD
CROSSING
2 TRACKS


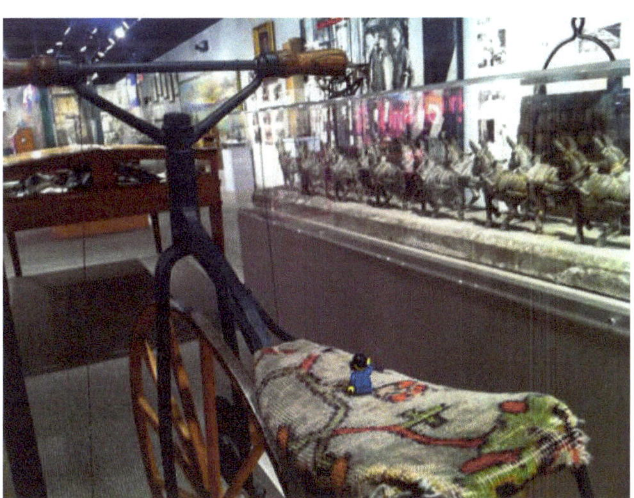

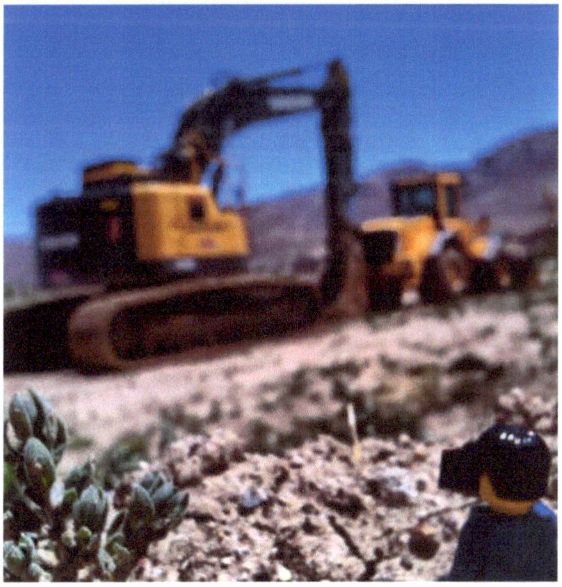

# HOLIDAYS

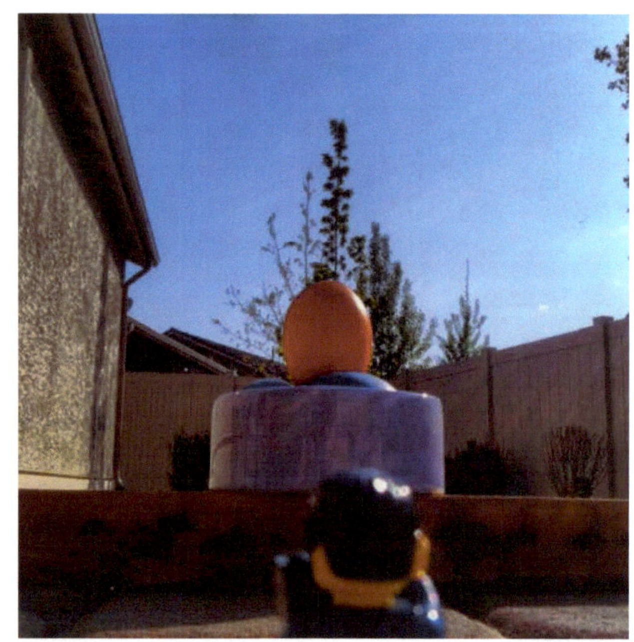

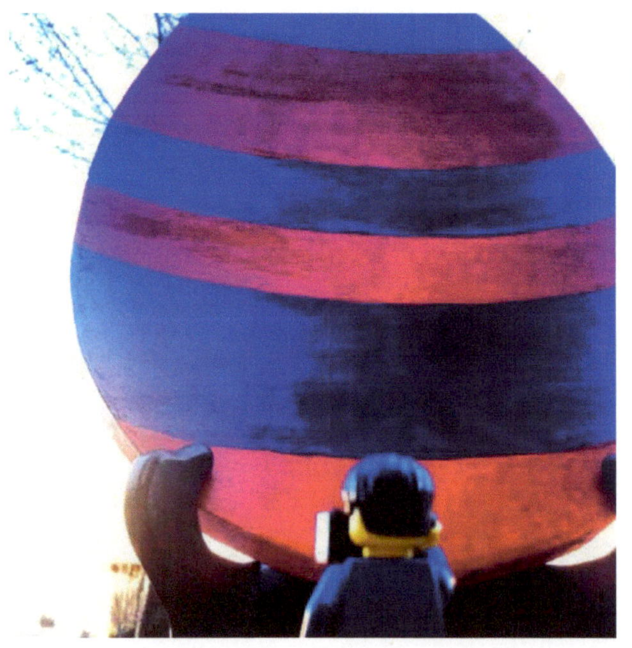

"Life should not only be lived.
It should be celebrated."
— Osho

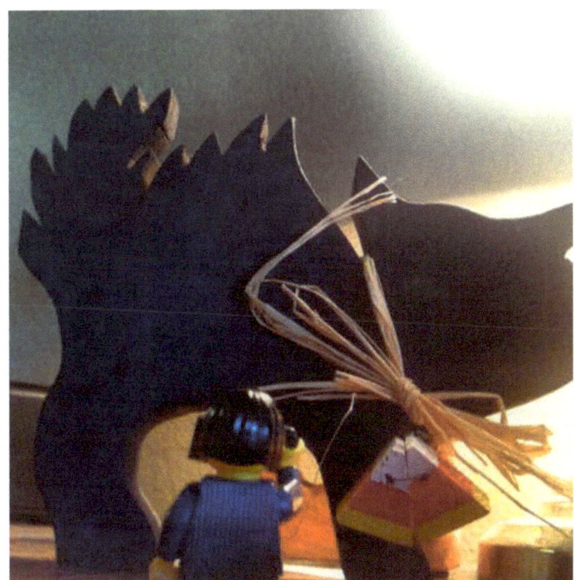

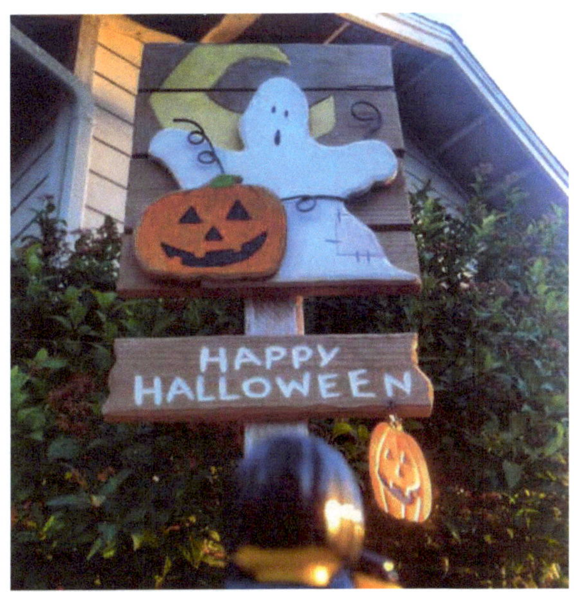

HAPPY
HALLOWEEN

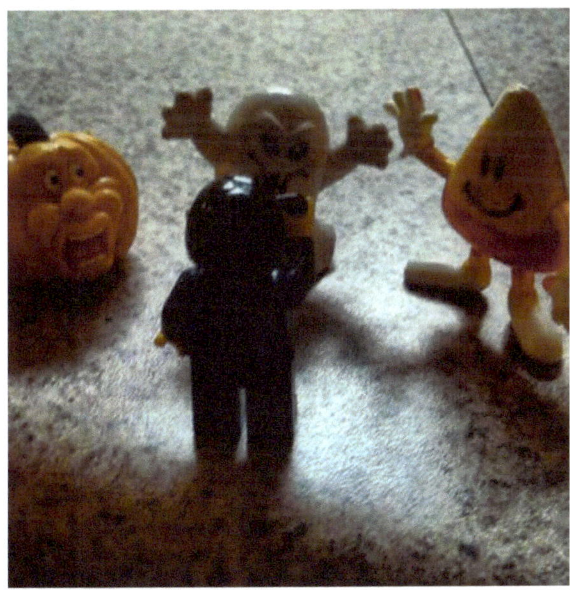

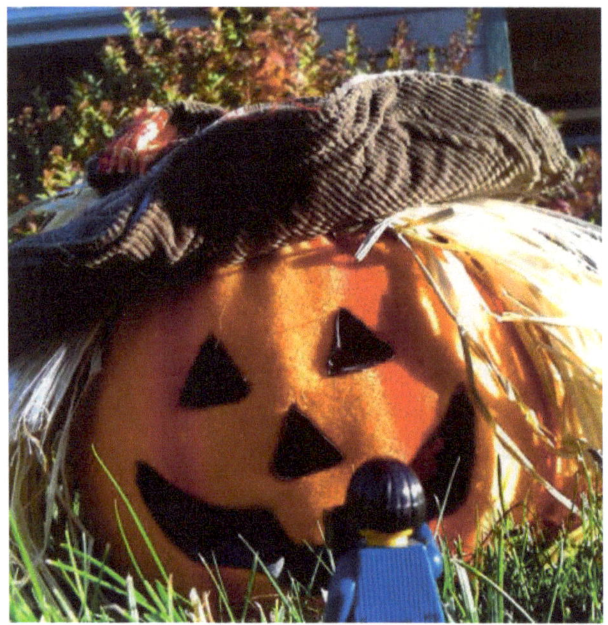

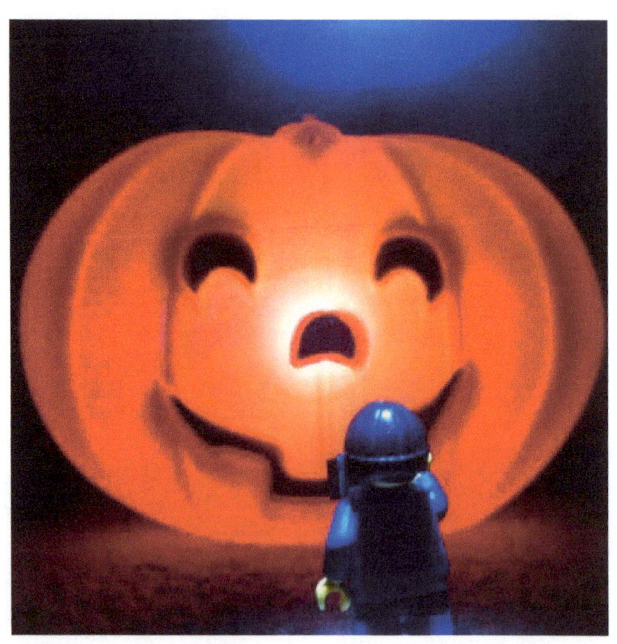

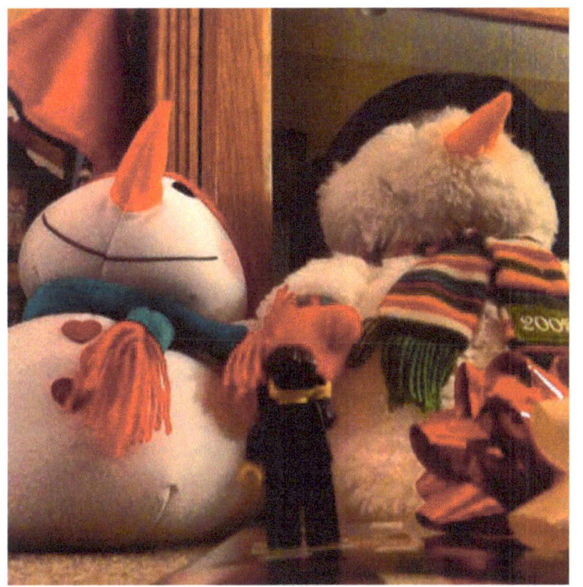

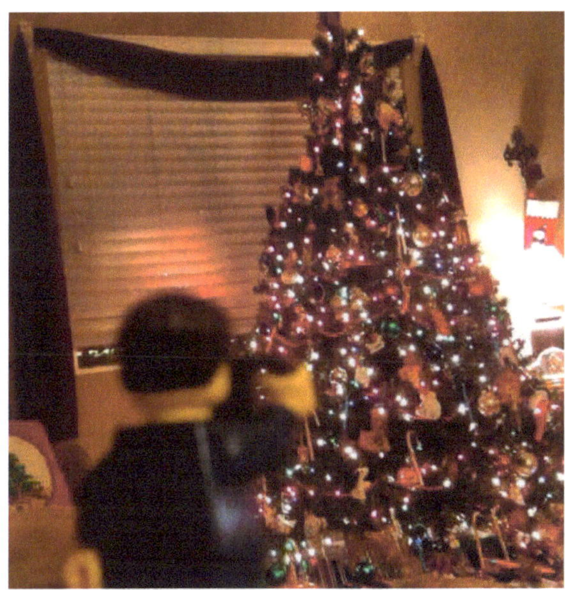

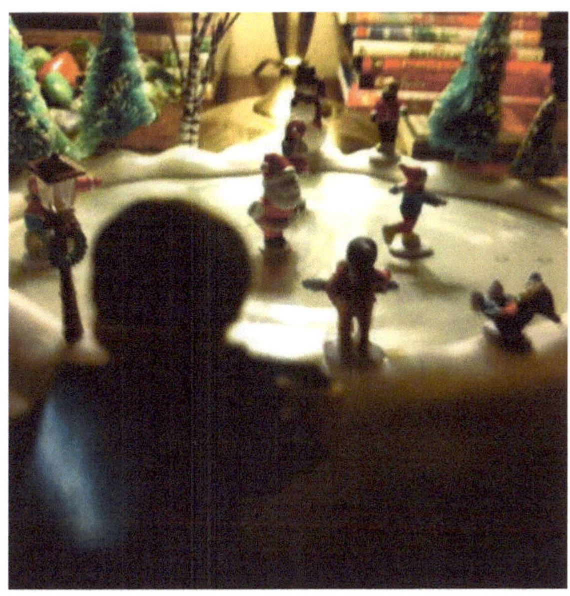

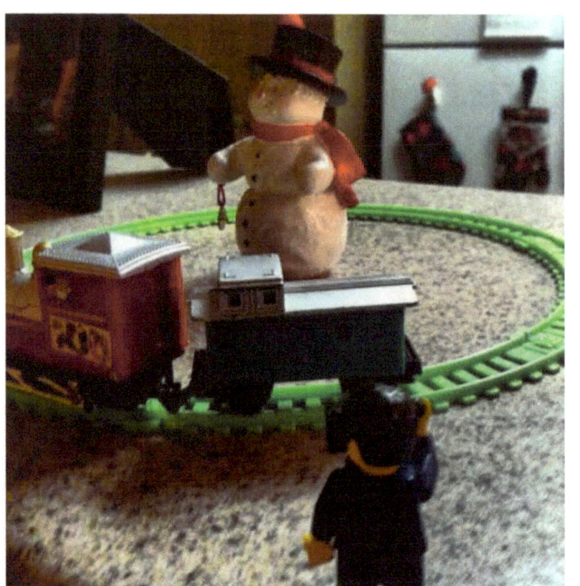

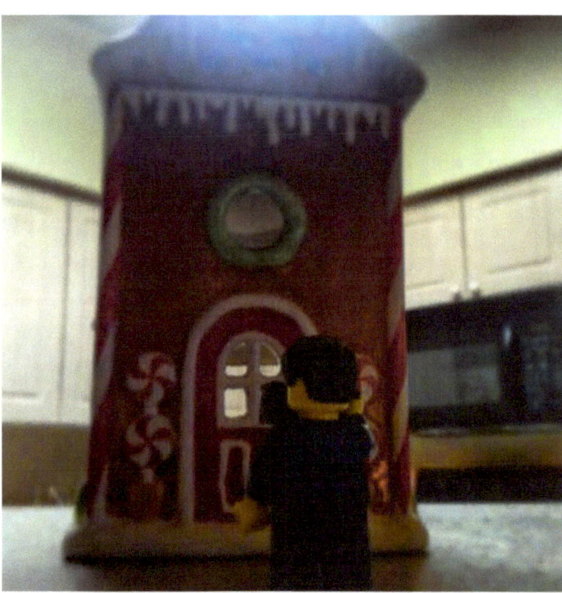

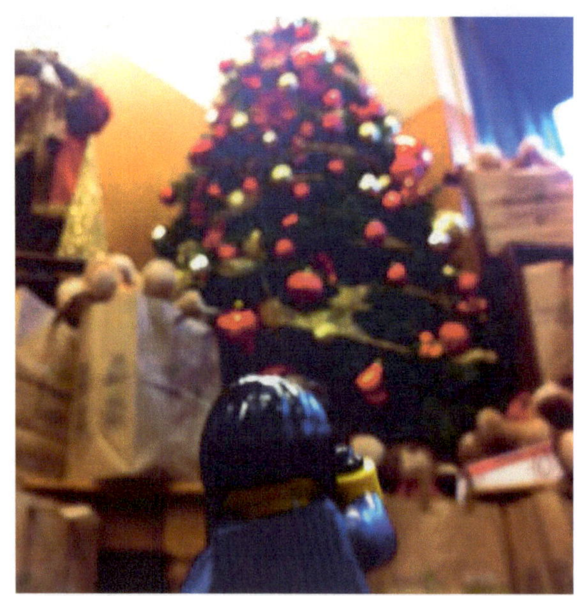

# EXPLORING AND DISCOVERING OUTDOORS

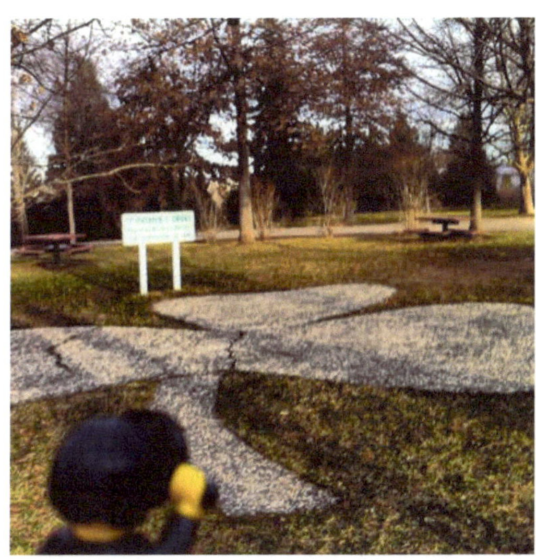

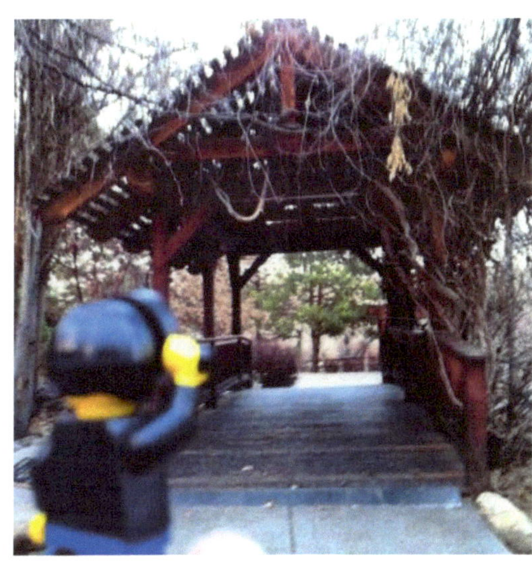

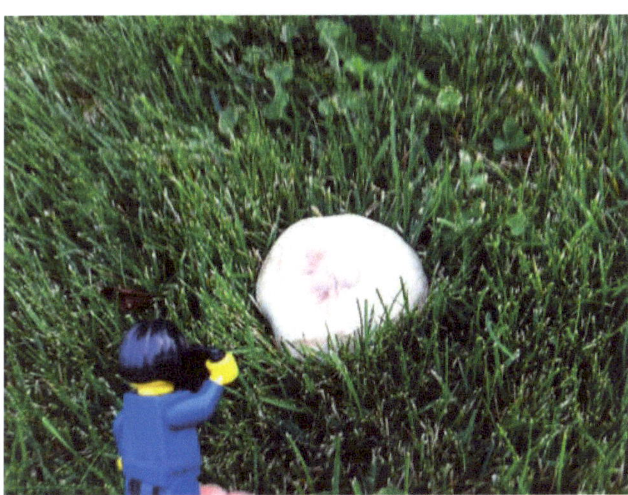

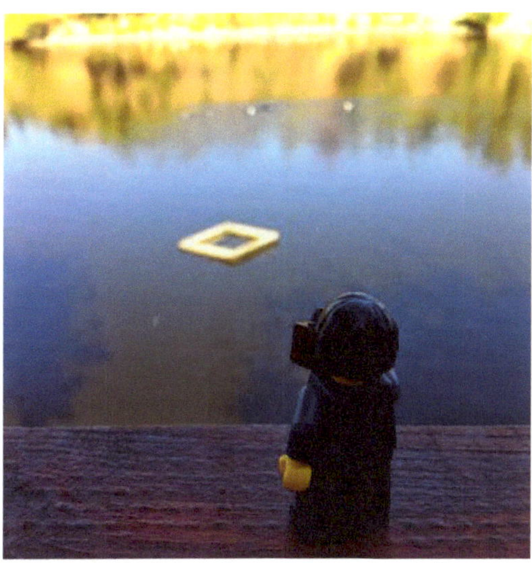

"It's not what you look at that matters. It's what you see."
— *Henry David Thoreau*

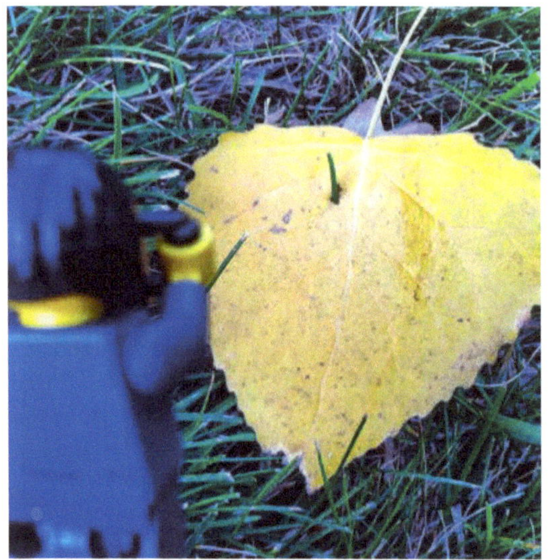

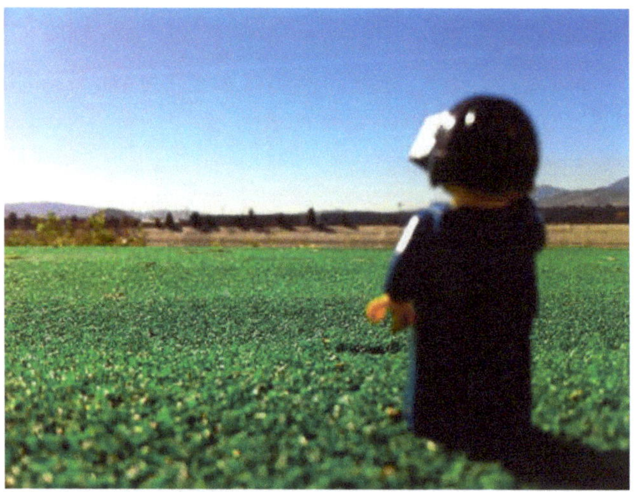

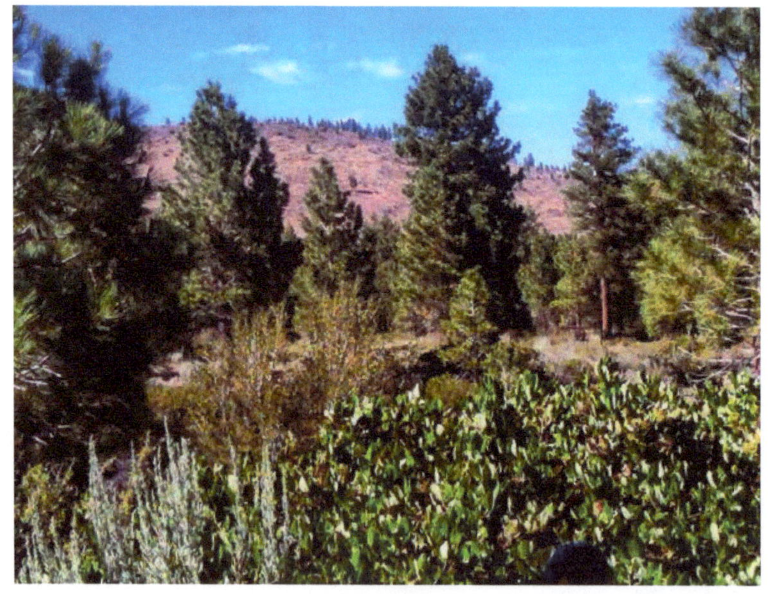

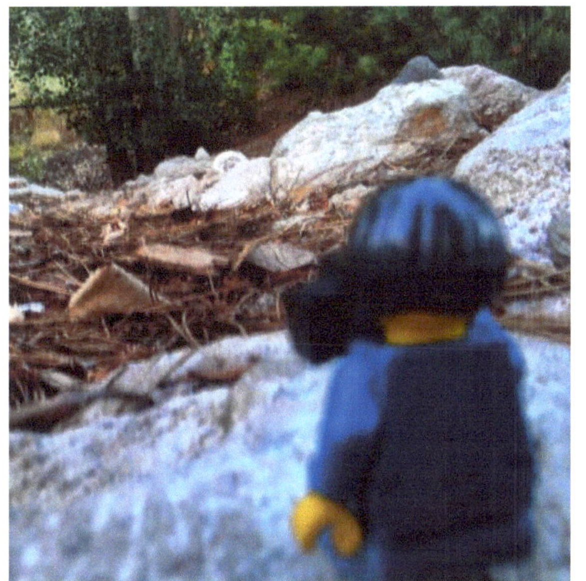

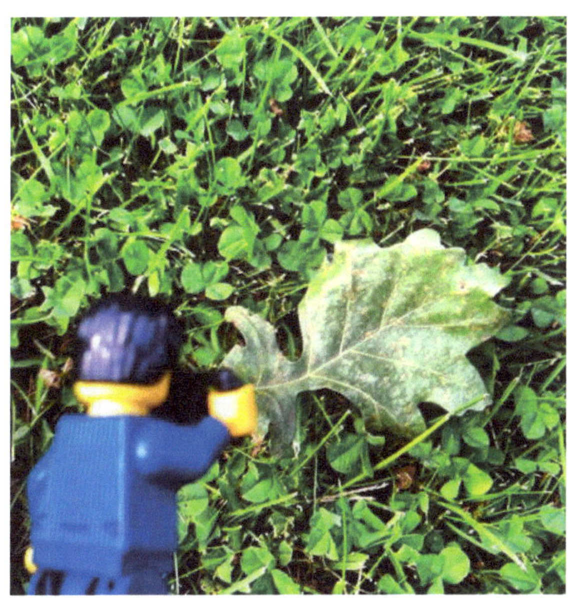

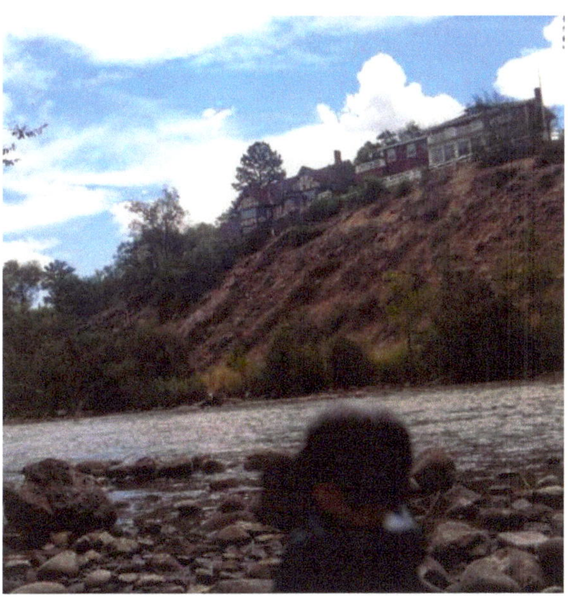

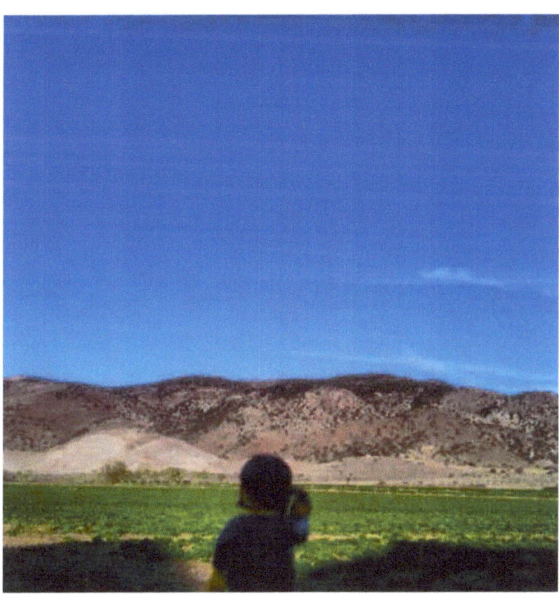

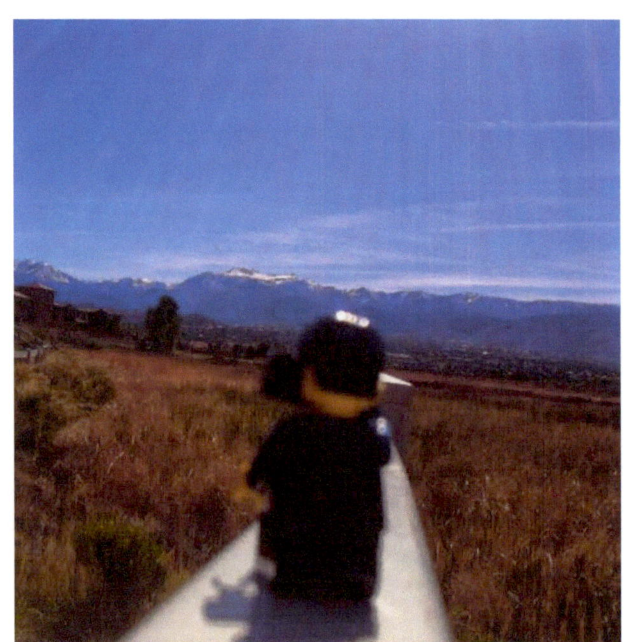

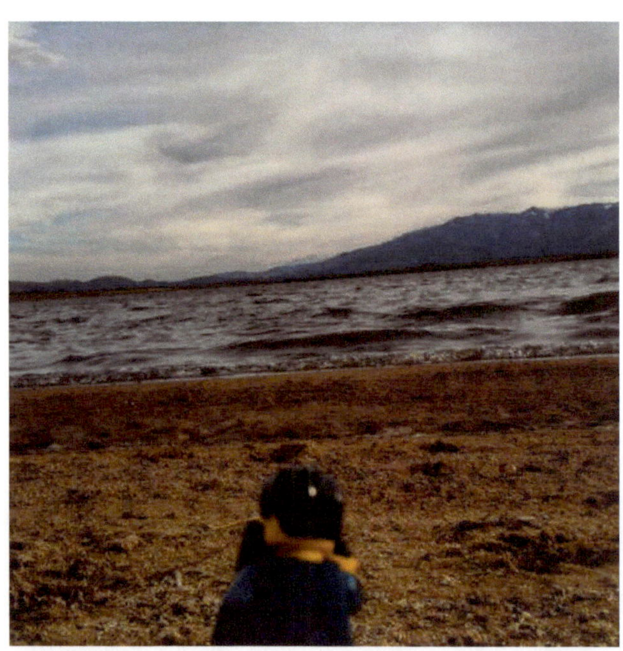

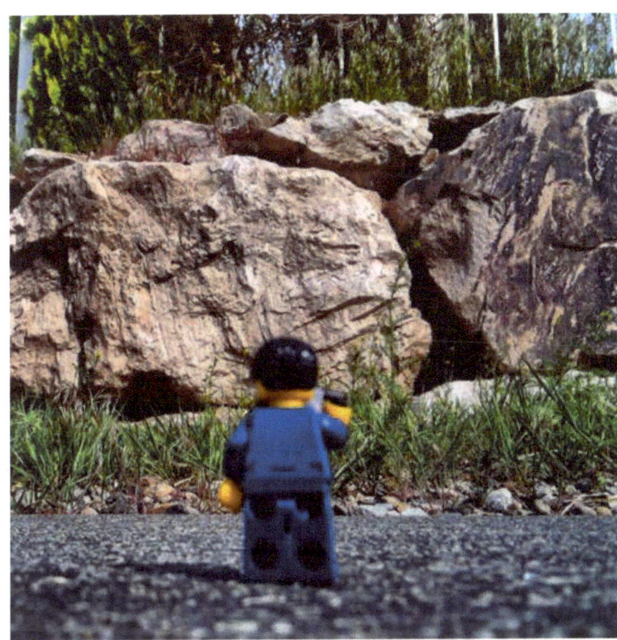

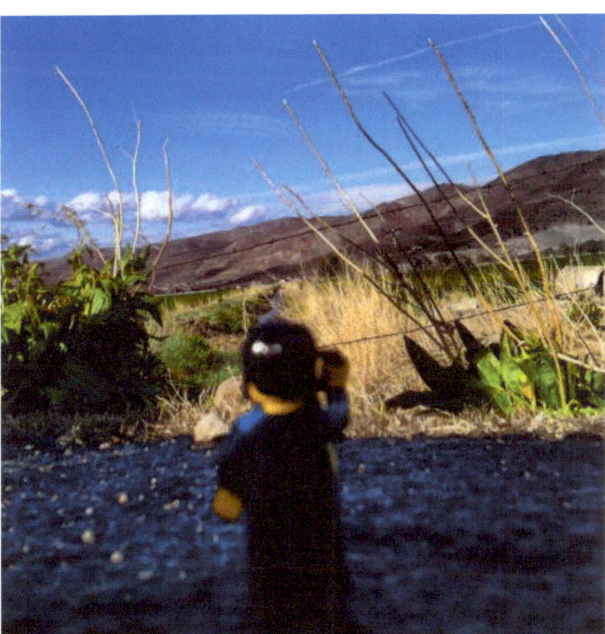

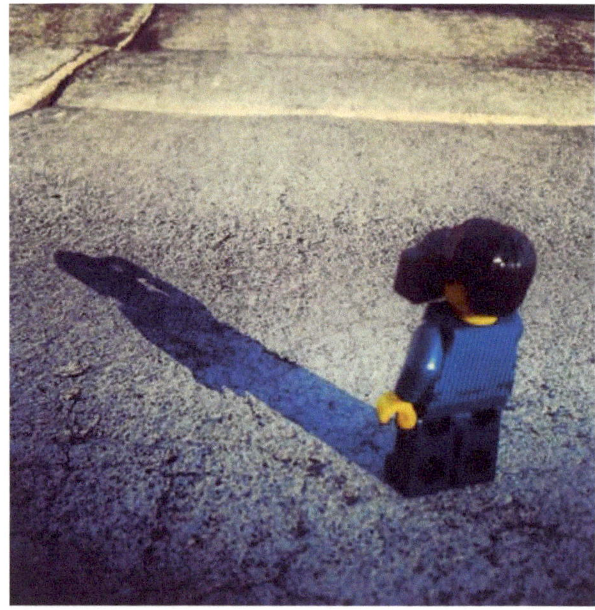

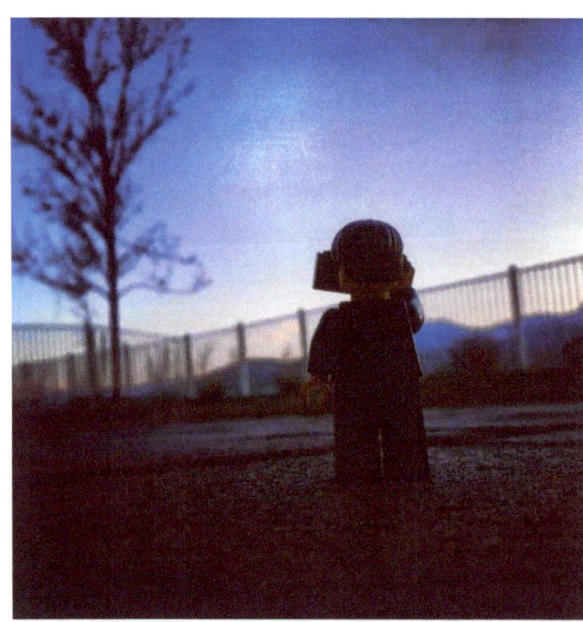

# GAMES, CELEBRATING, AND FUN!

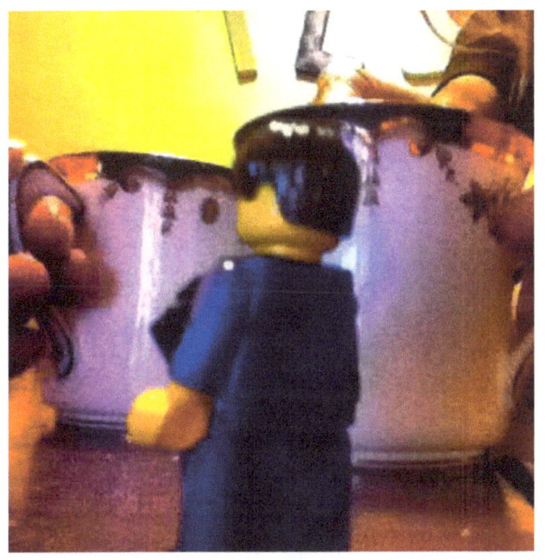

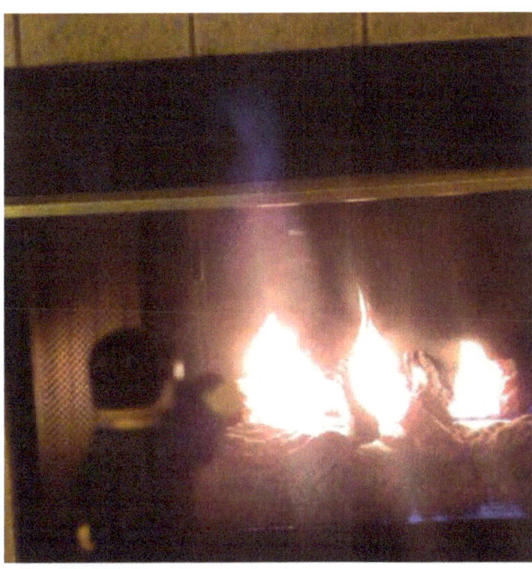

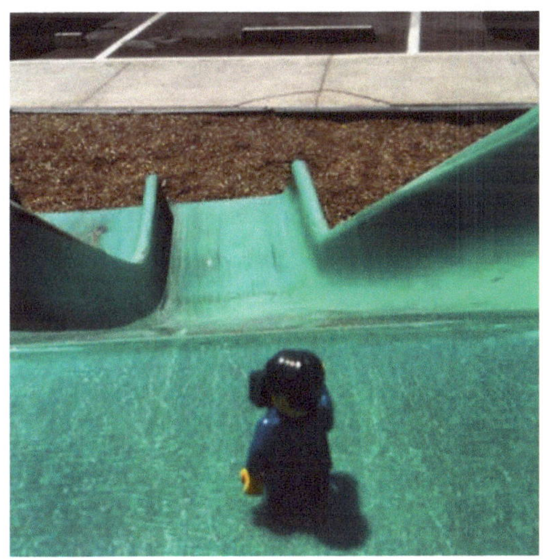

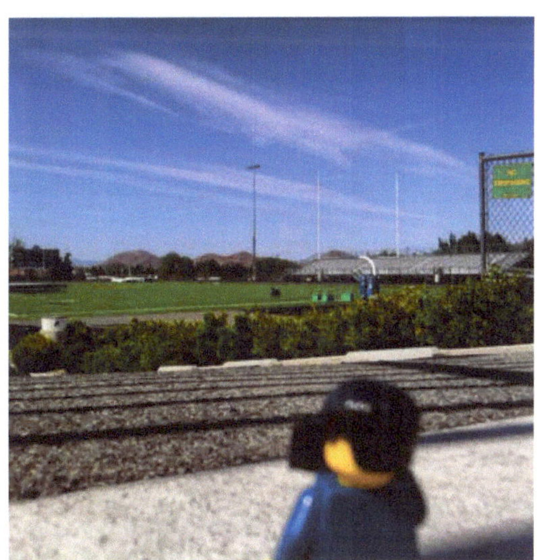

"Today was good. Today was fun. Tomorrow is another one."
— *Dr. Seuss*

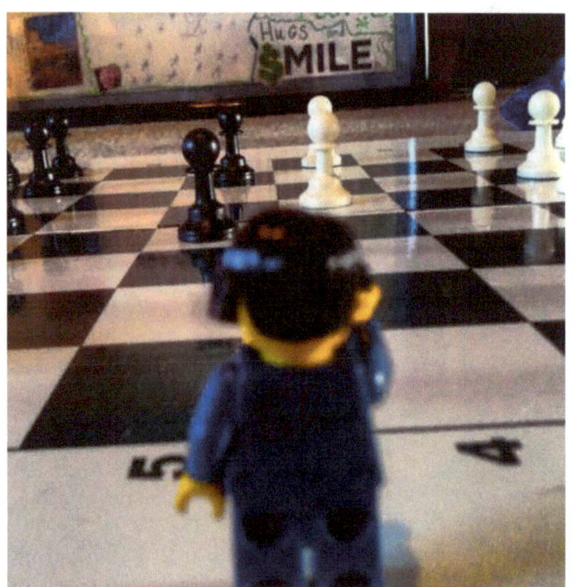

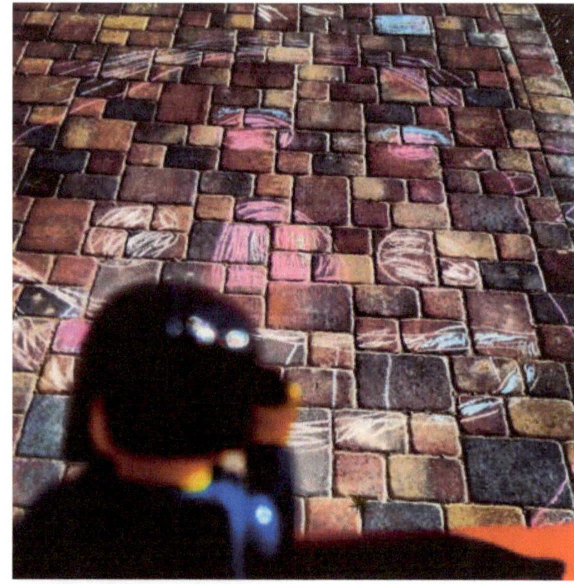

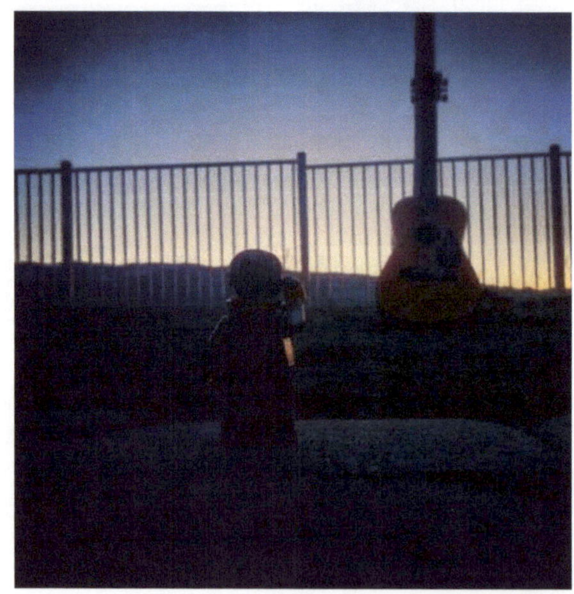

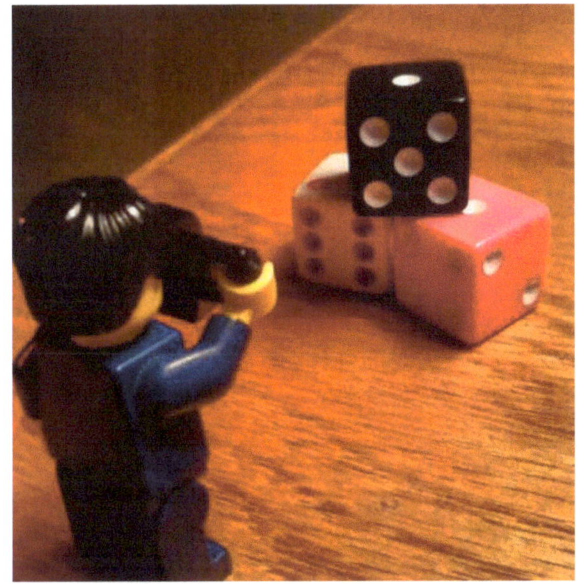

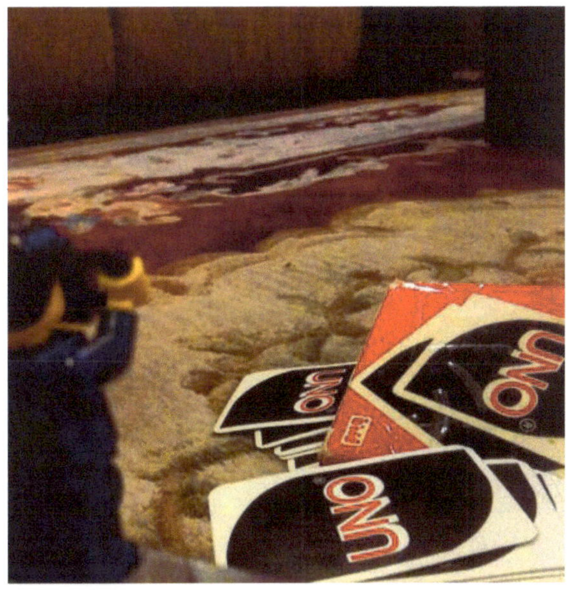

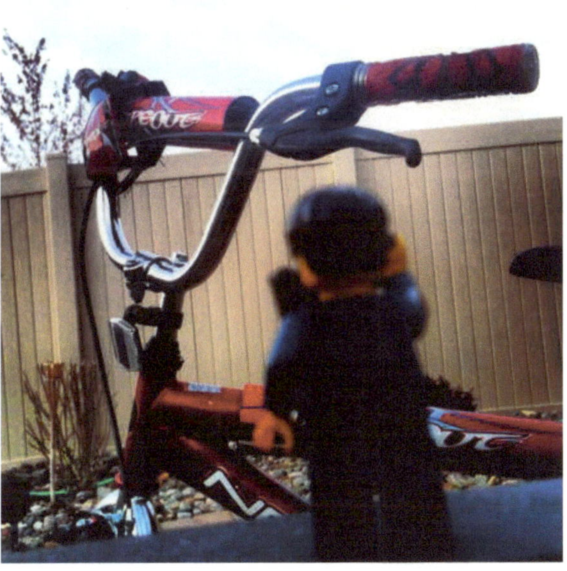

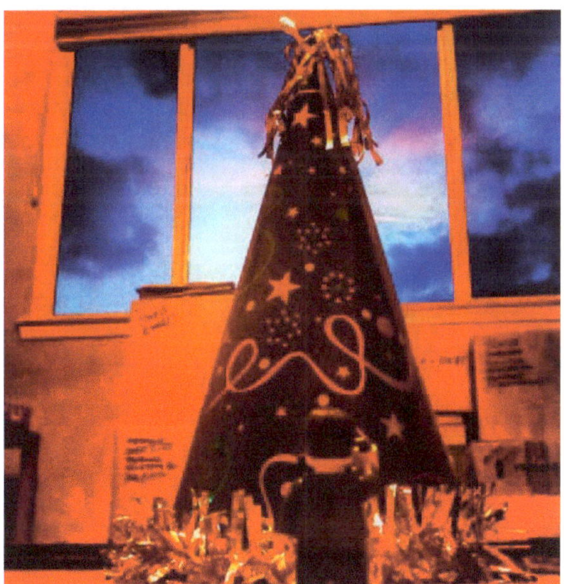

# TREES!

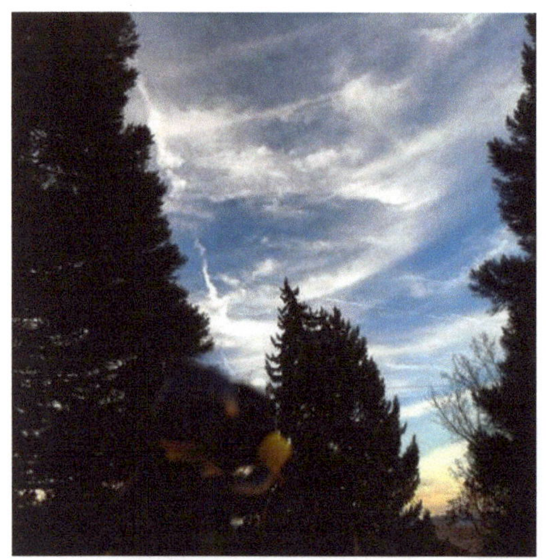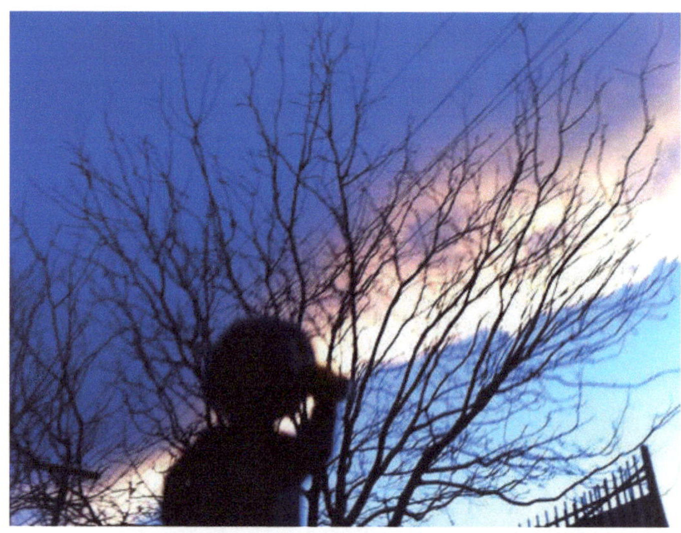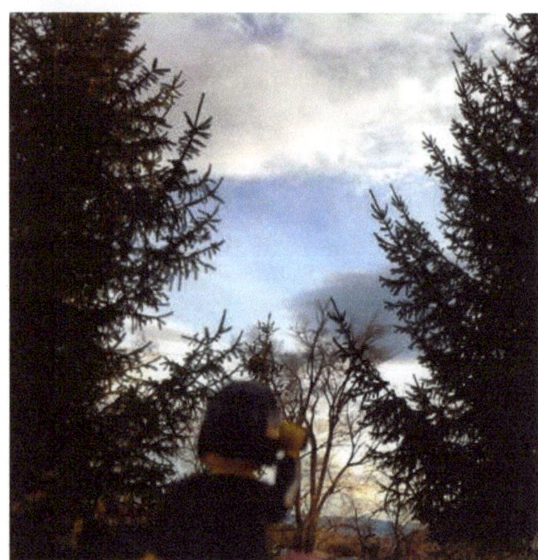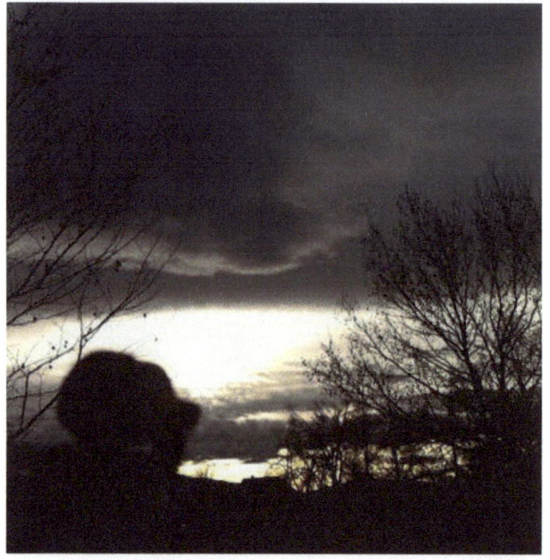

"The winds blow their own freshness into you, and the storms their energy, while cares will drop off like autumn leaves."     — *John Muir*

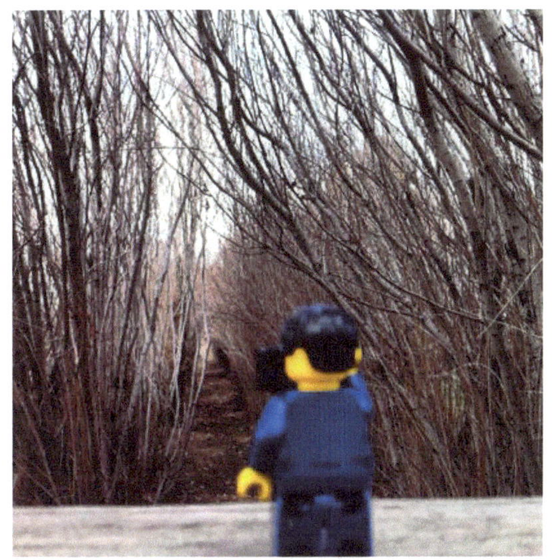

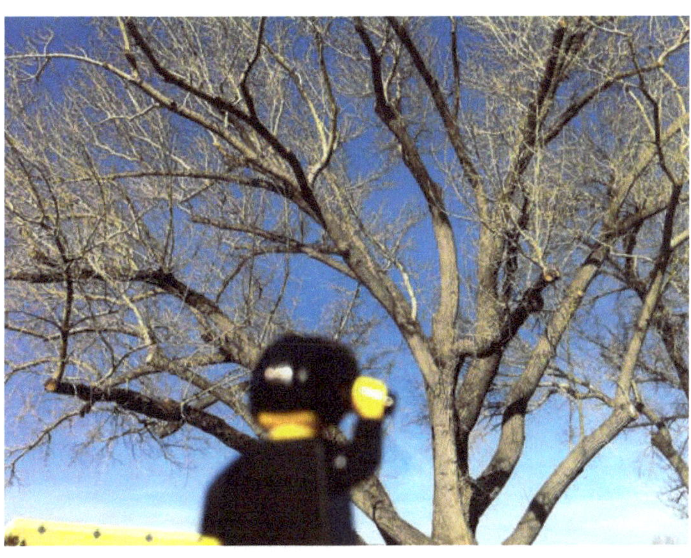

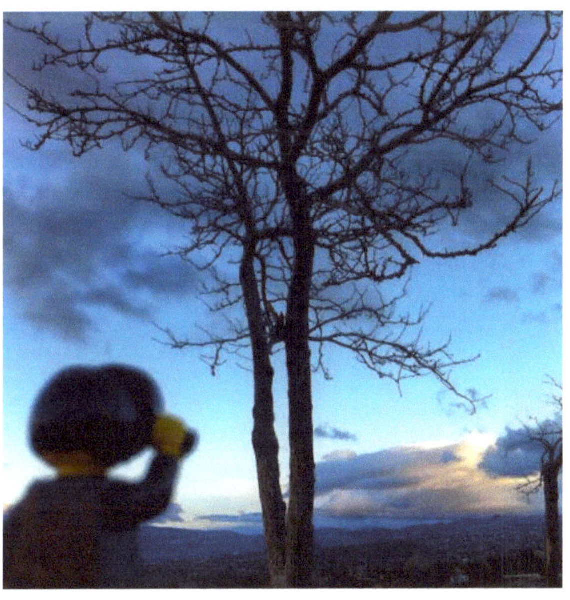

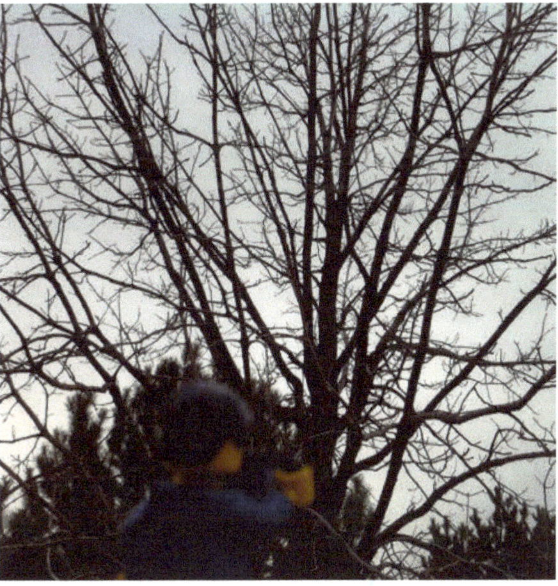

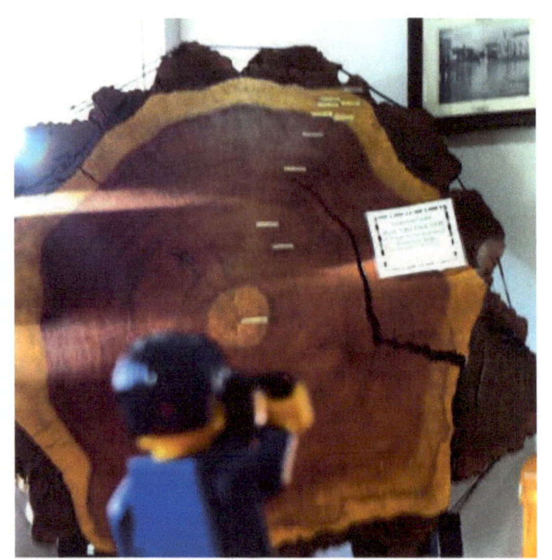

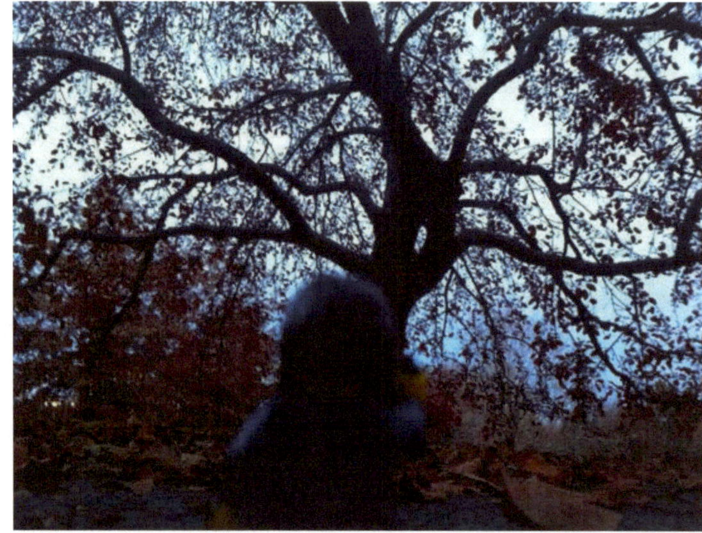

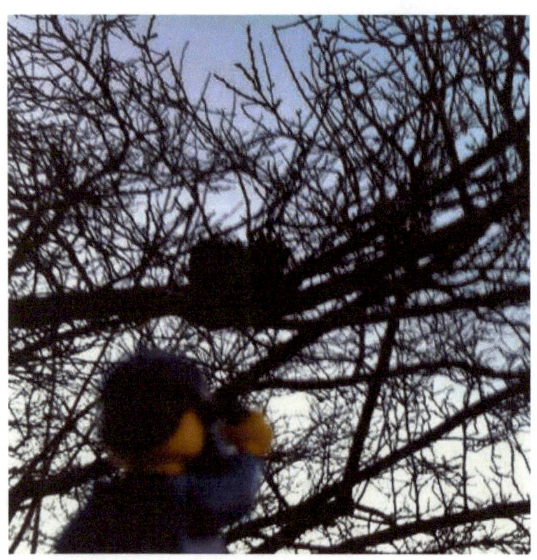

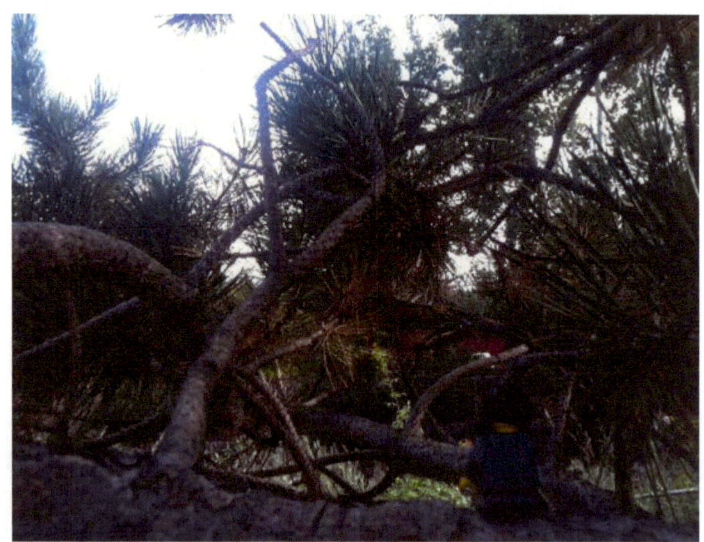

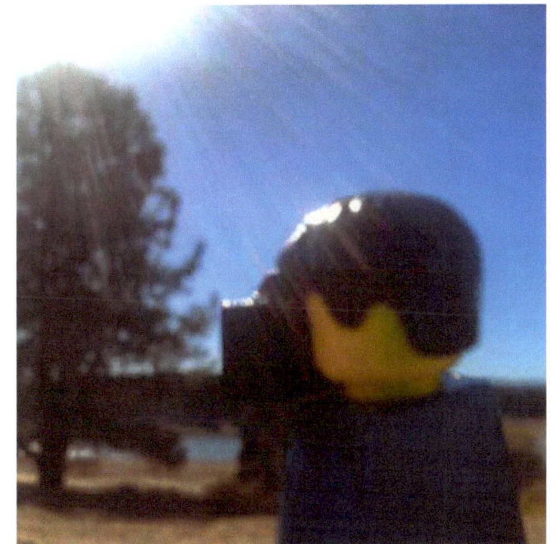

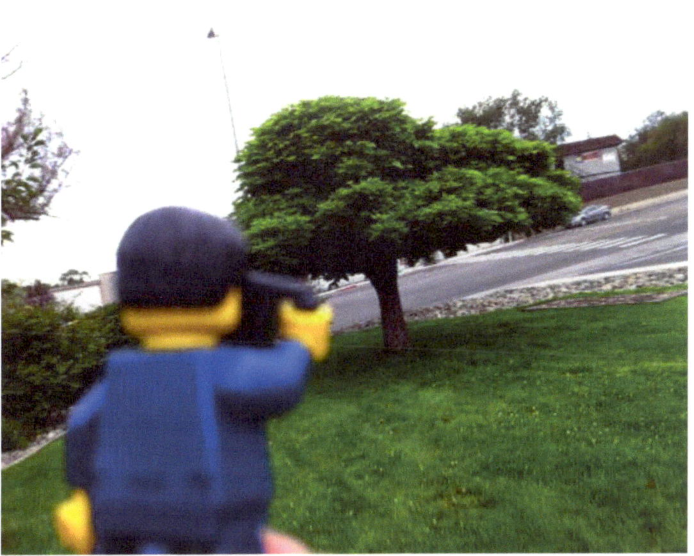

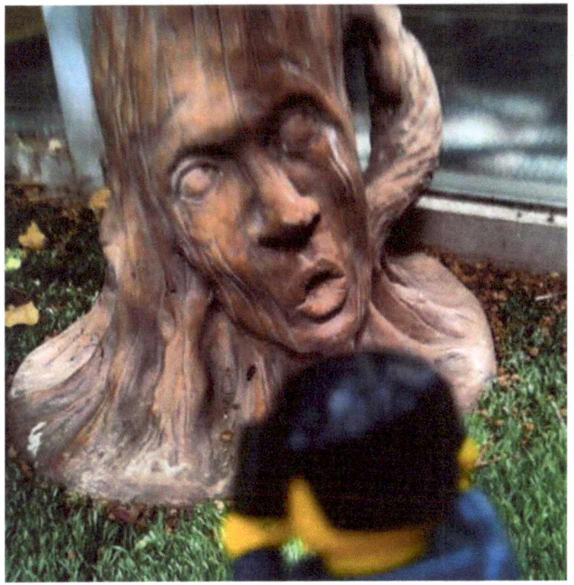

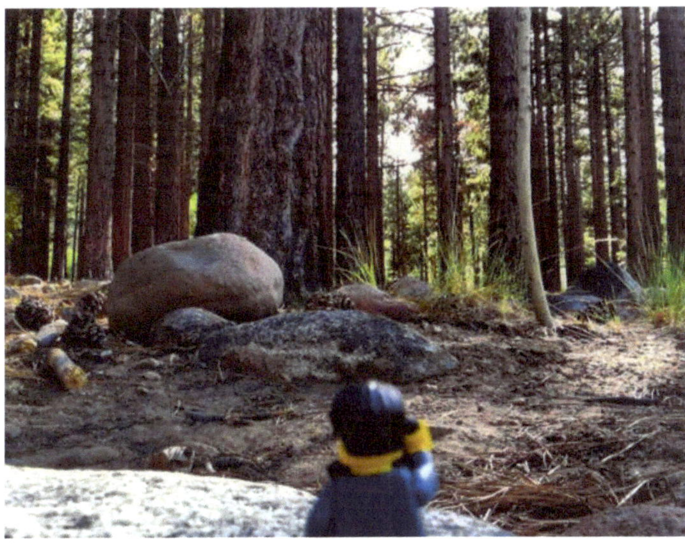

# TRIP TO STAMFORD, CONNECTICUT FOR THE 2014 CHROMOSOME 18 REGISTRY & RESEARCH SOCIETY FAMILY CONFERENCE

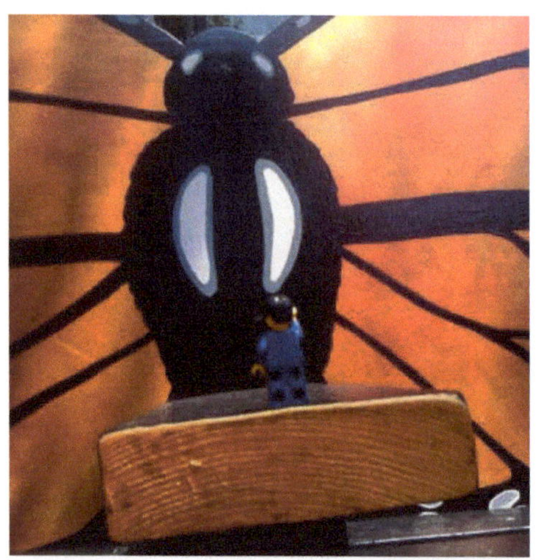

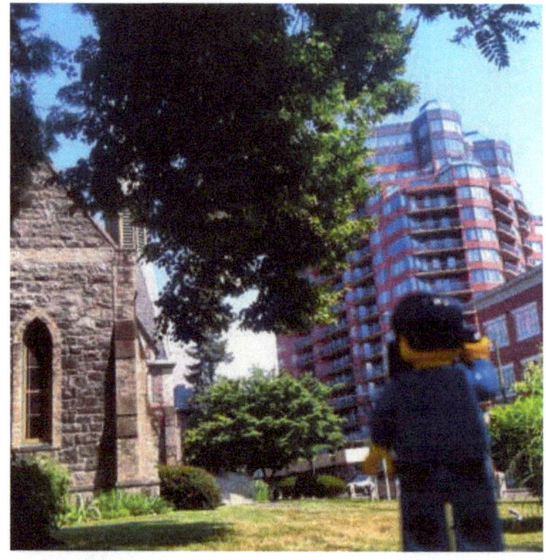

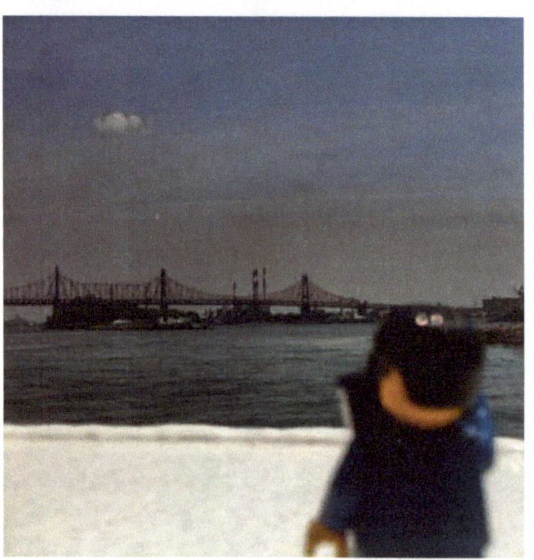

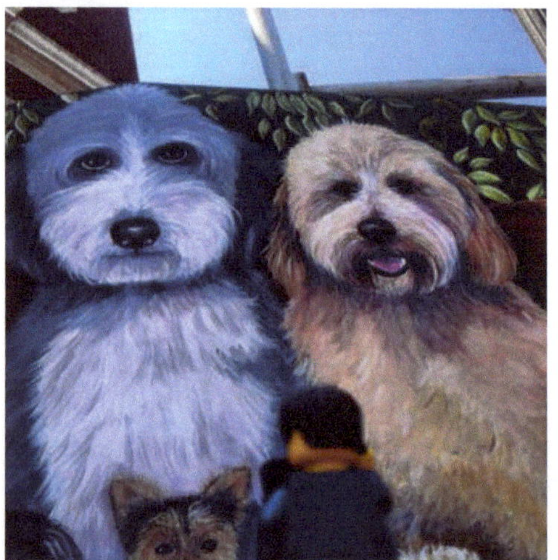

"Do what you can, with what you have, where you are."
— Theodore Roosevelt

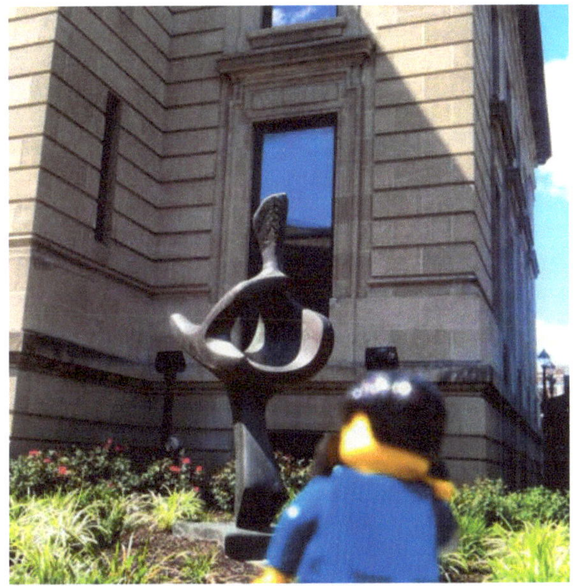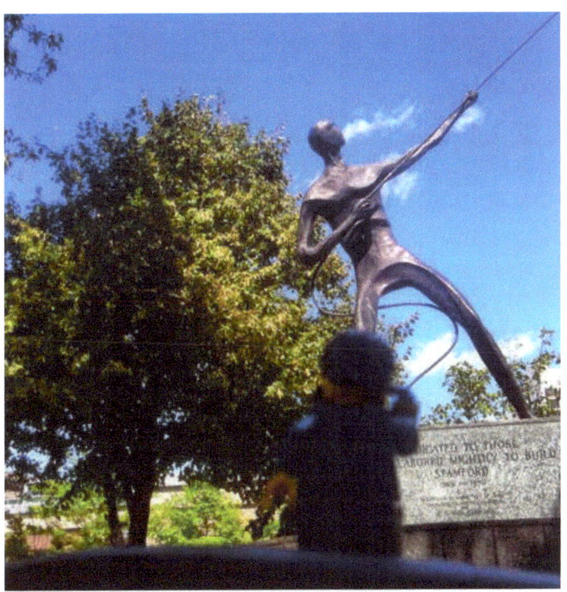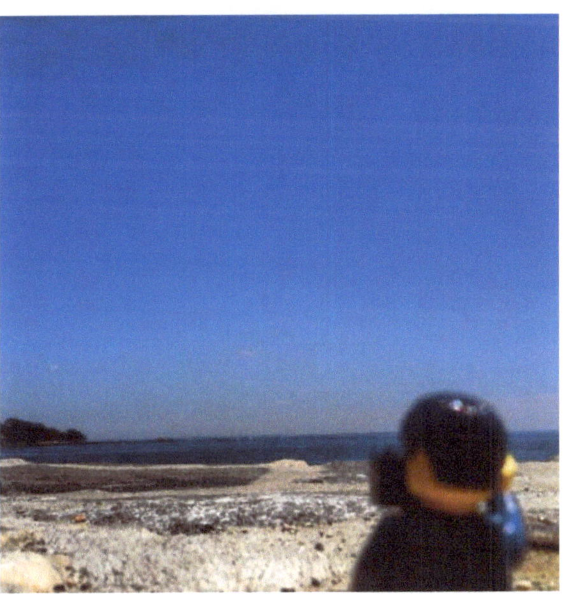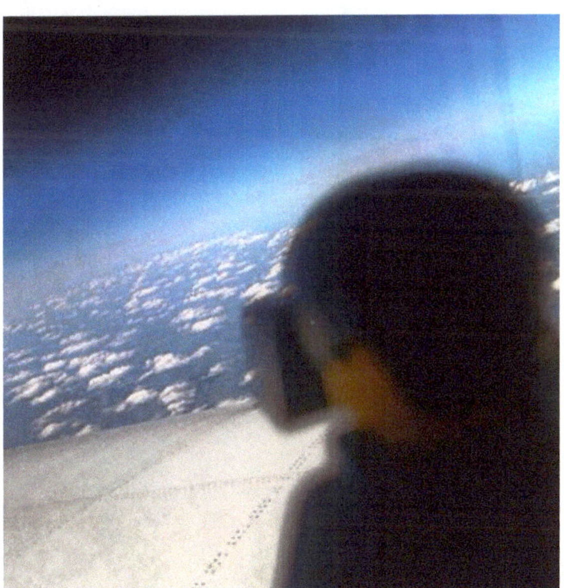

*Thomas Darnell*

# Expressions of the Sky, Sunset, and Clouds

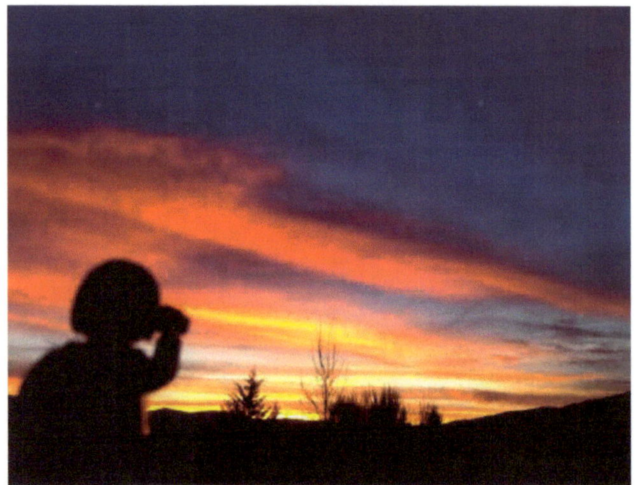
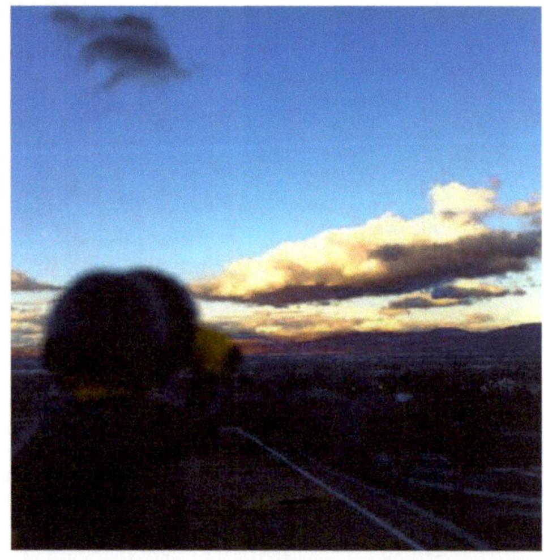
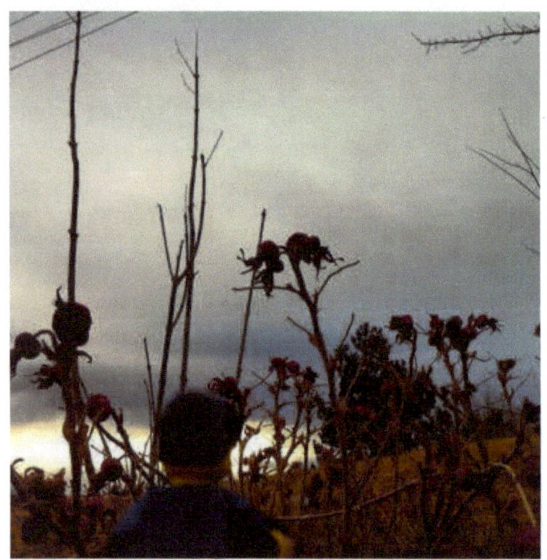
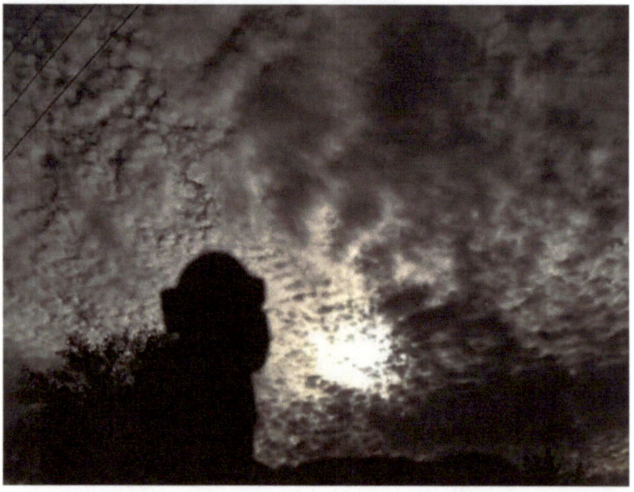

"Those who contemplate the beauty of the earth find reserves of strength that will endure as long as life lasts. There is something infinitely healing in the repeated refrains of nature -- the assurance that dawn comes after night, and spring after winter."
— *Rachel Carson*

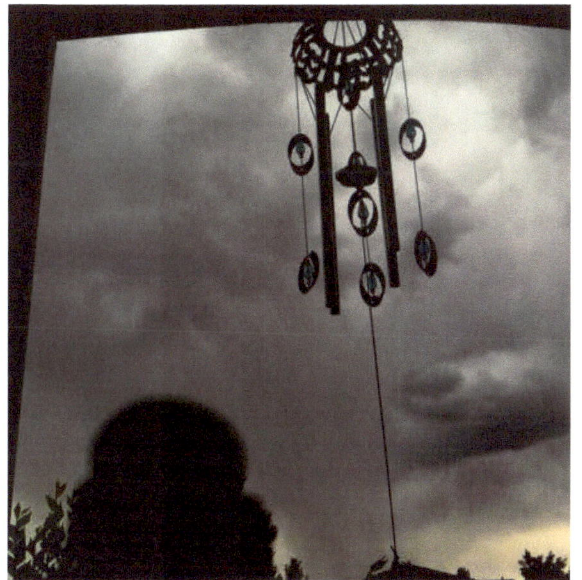

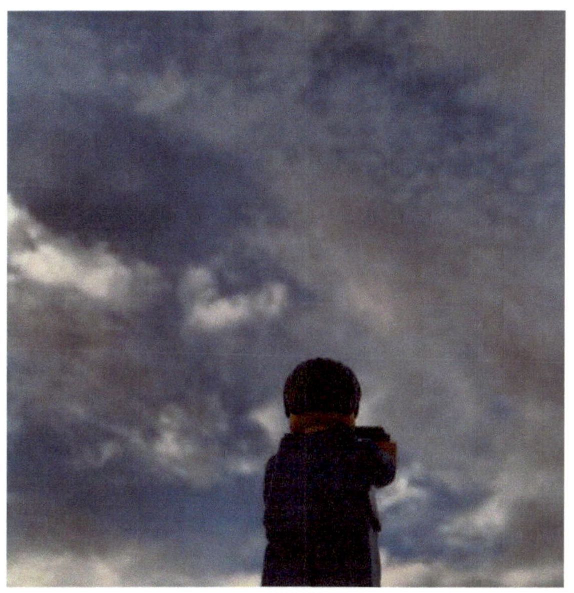

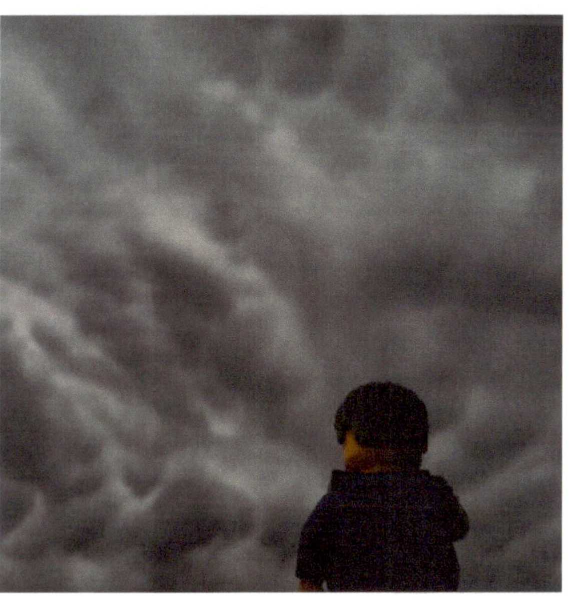

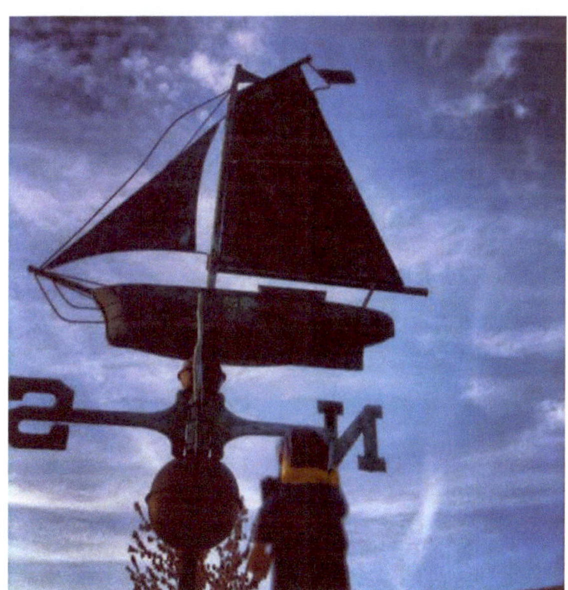

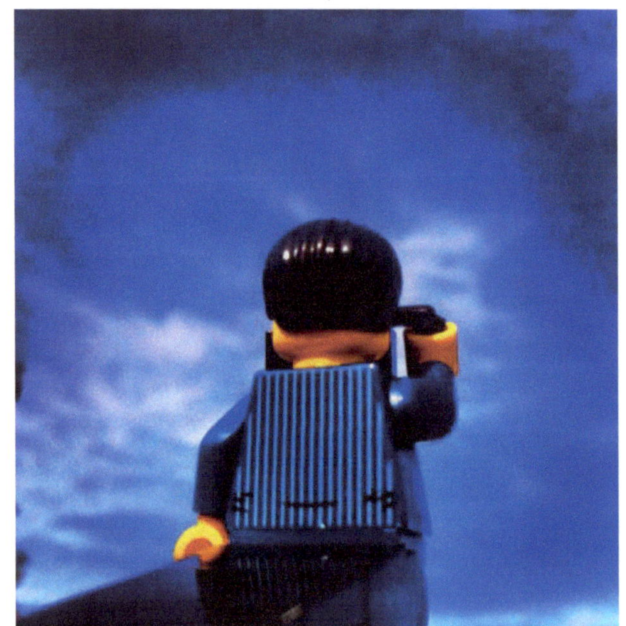

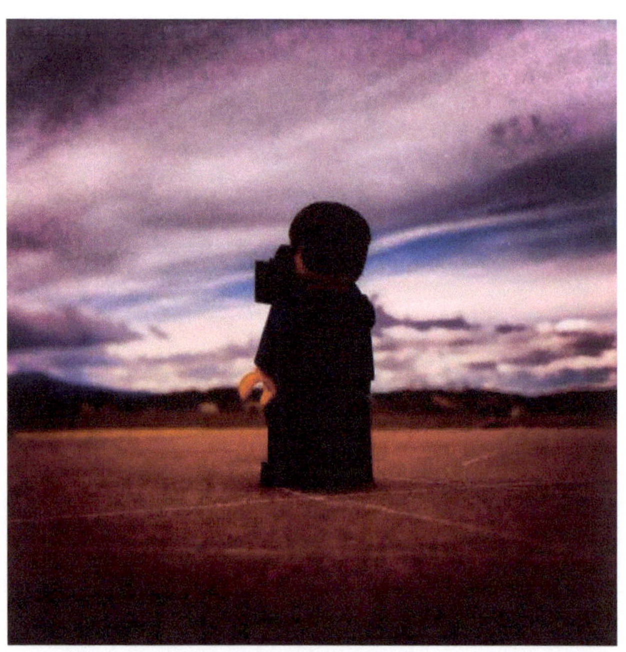

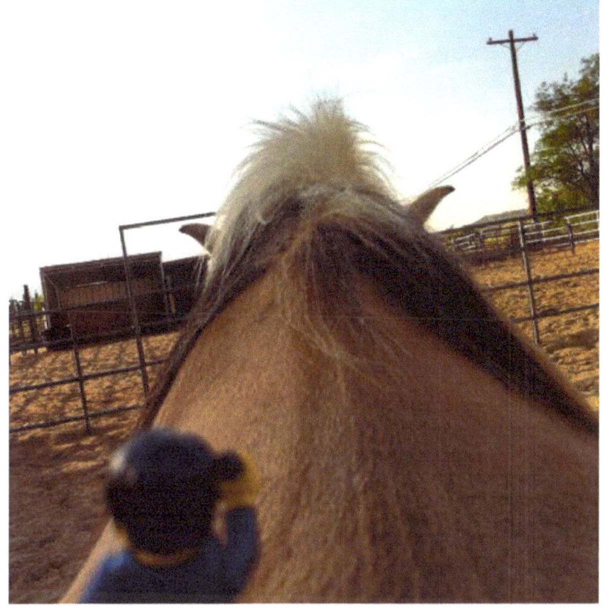

# HORSE LOVE AT BARB'S PLACE - STARRING MEG AND BUTTERCUP

"Until one has loved an animal, a part of one's soul remains unawakened."

— Anatole France

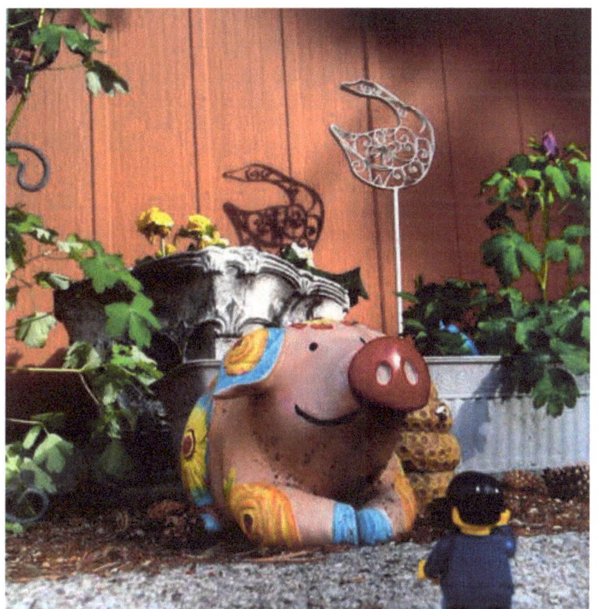

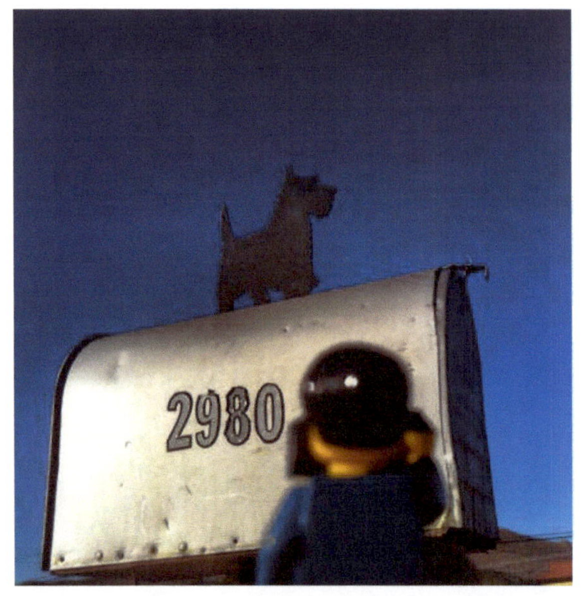

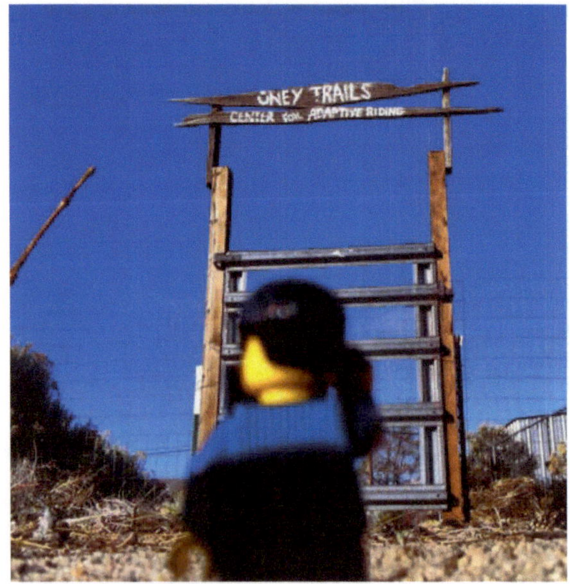

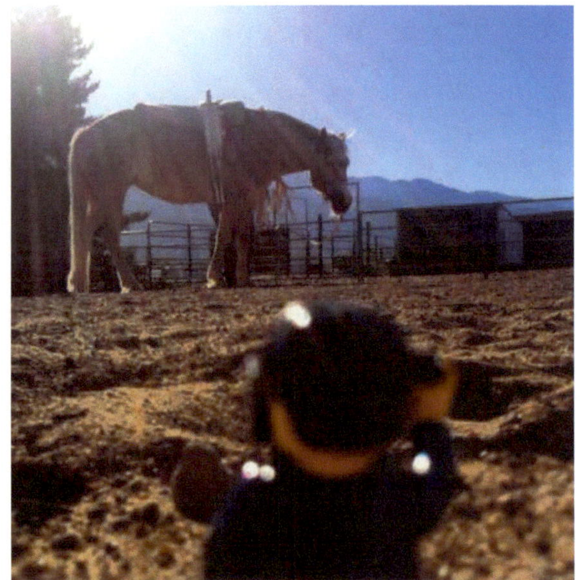

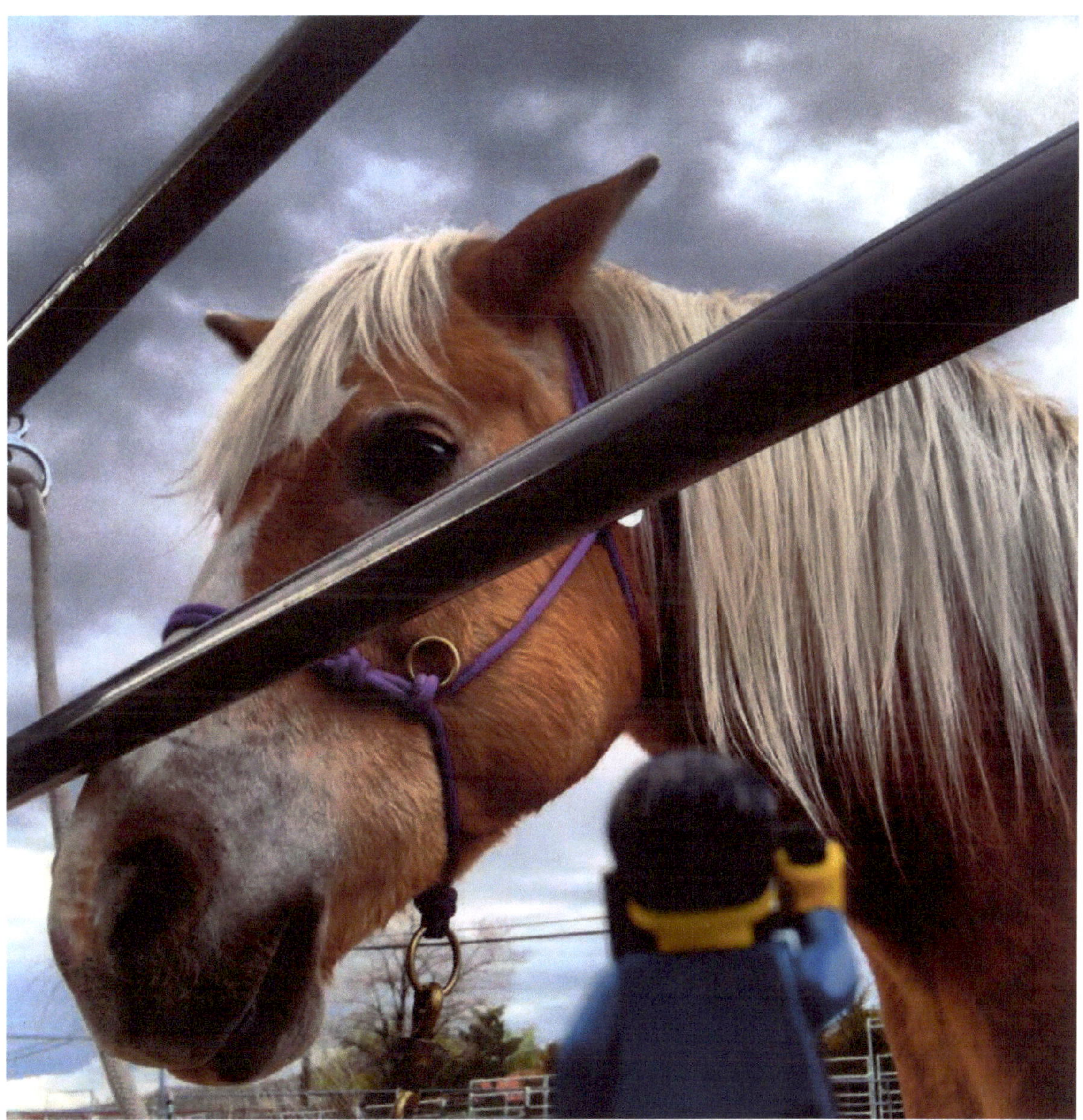

# ANIMAL ADVENTURES!

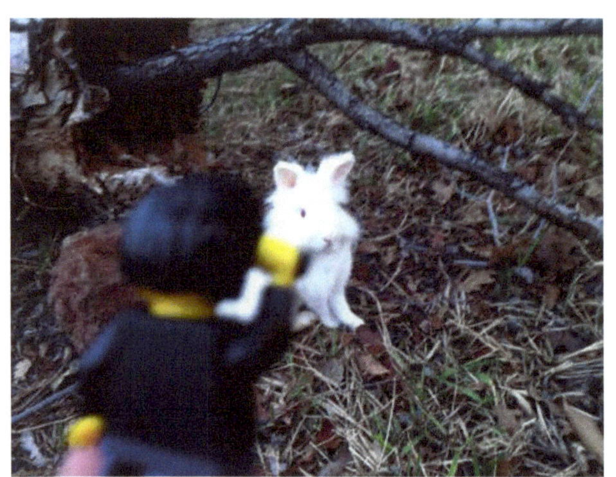

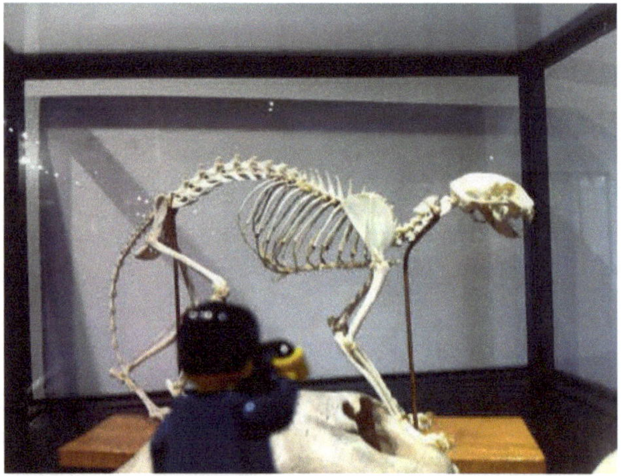

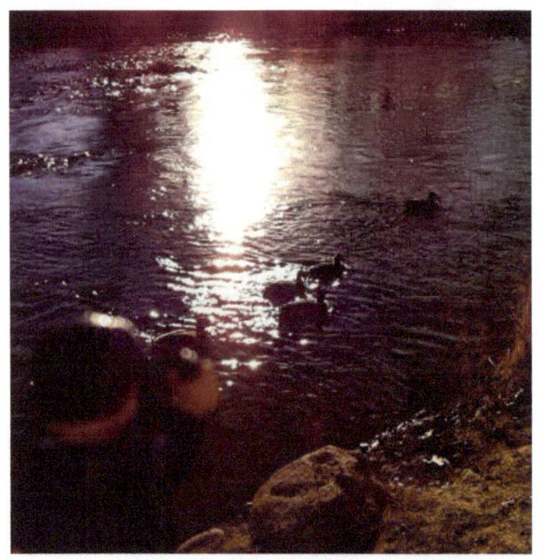

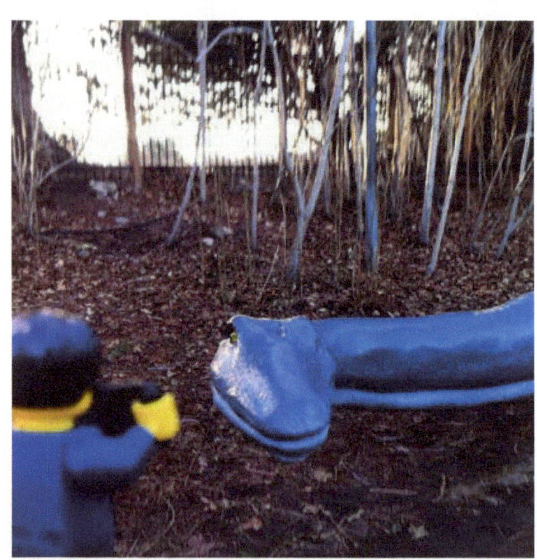

"Not all those who wander are lost"
— *J.R.R. Tolkien*

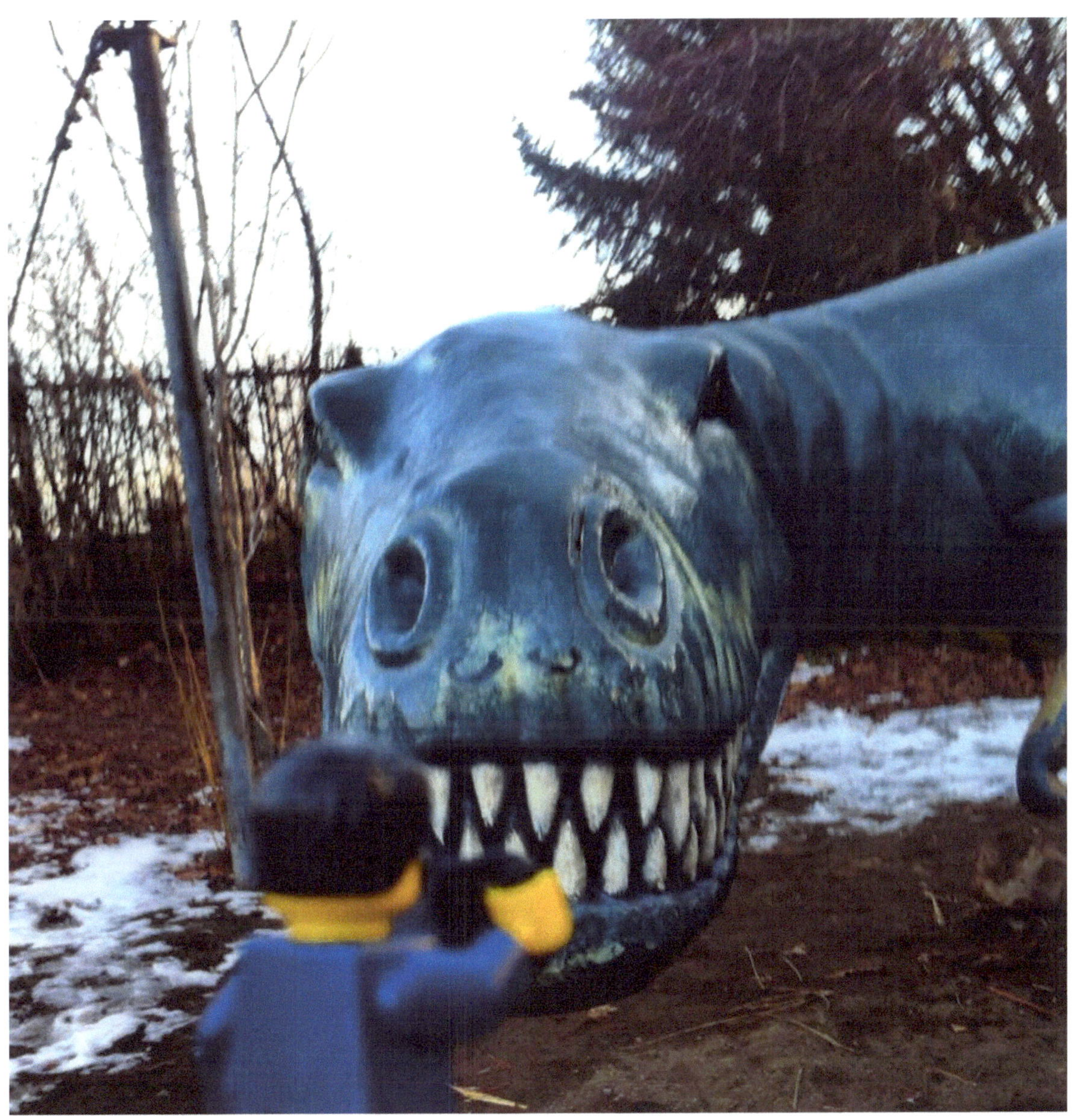

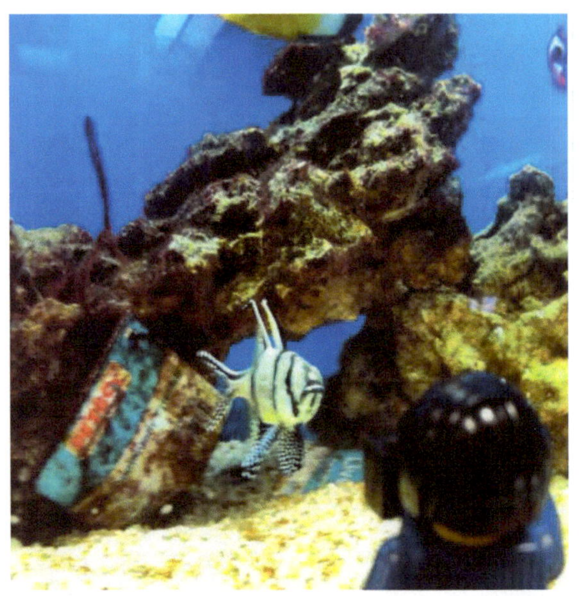
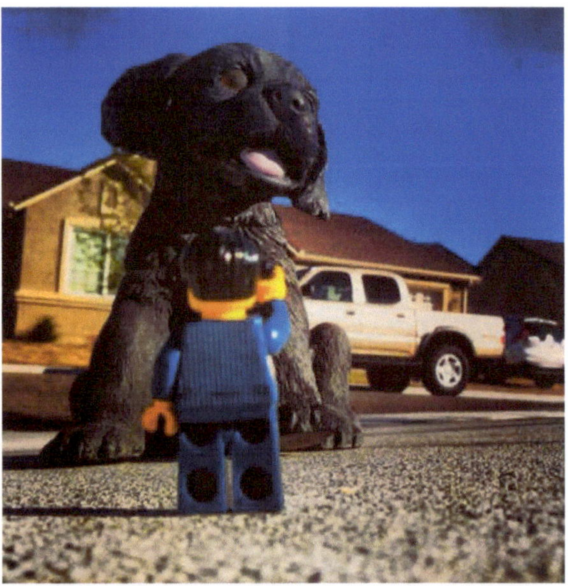
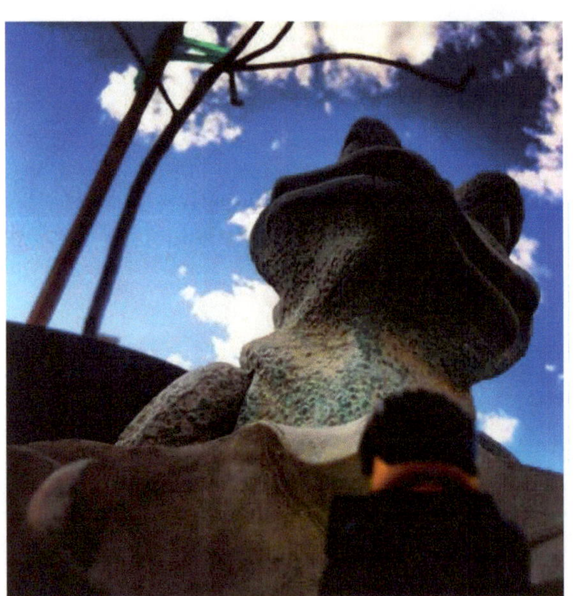
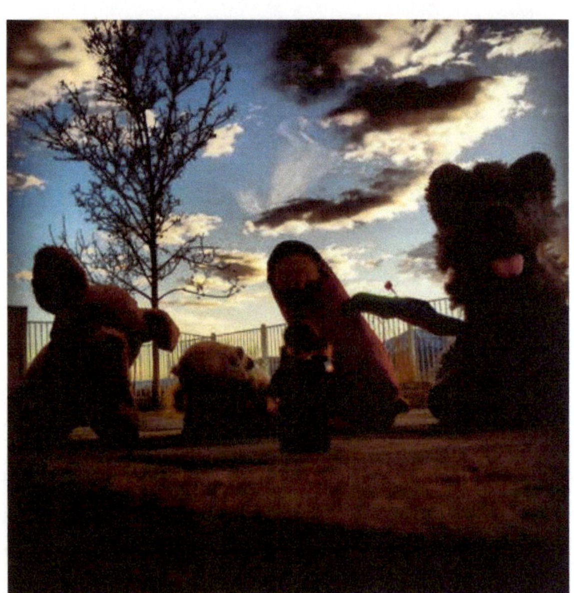

# FLOWERS AND FOUNTAINS!

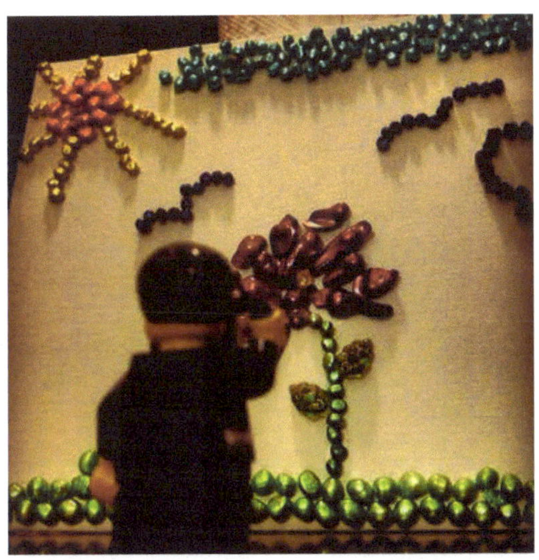

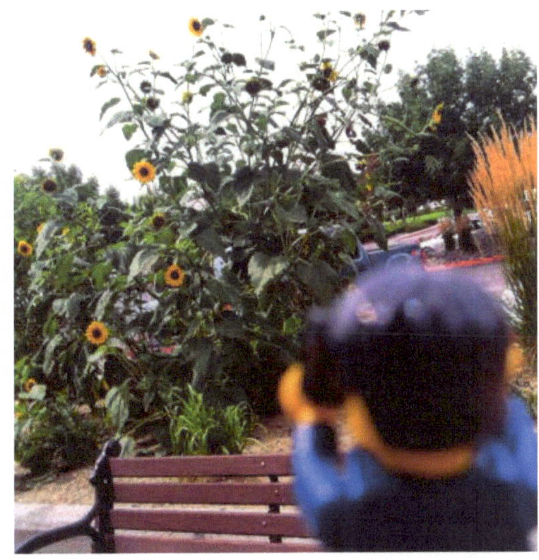

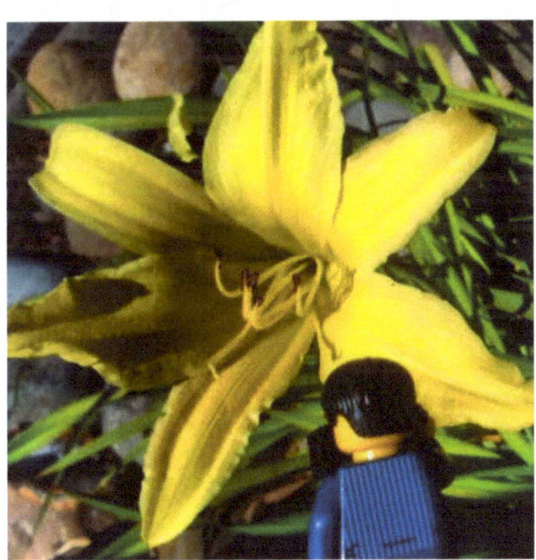

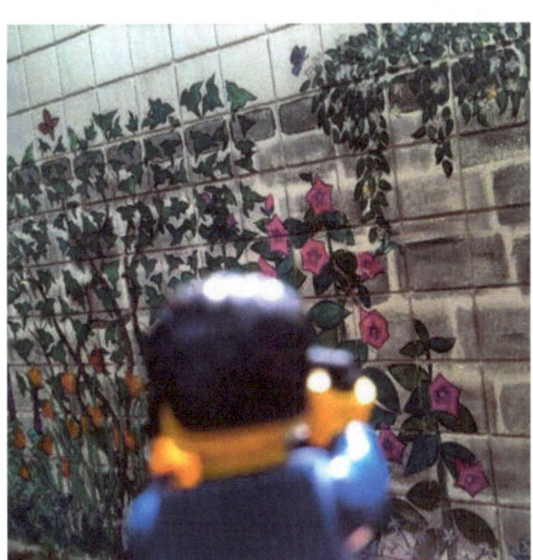

"Nature, like an enthusiastic gardner, could not resist the temptation to plant flowers everywhere."

— *John Muir*

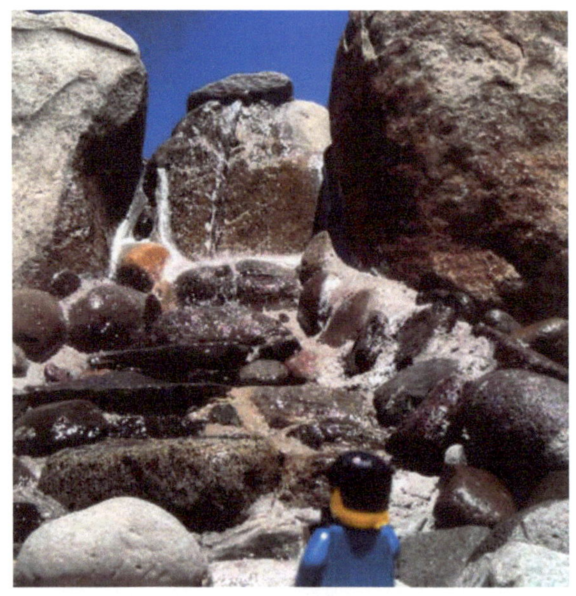
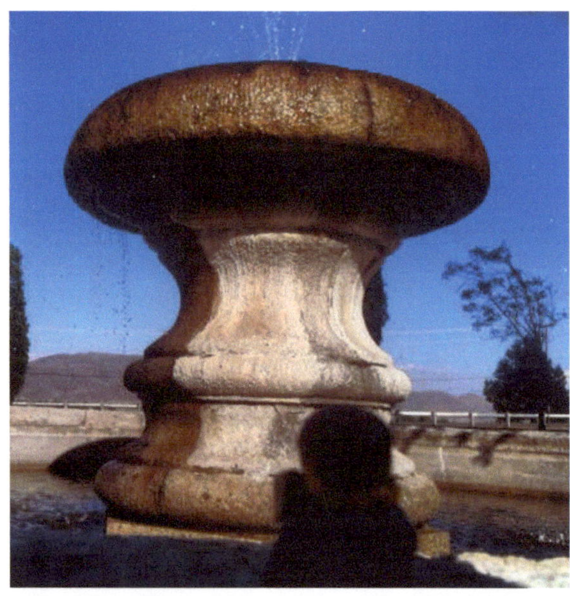
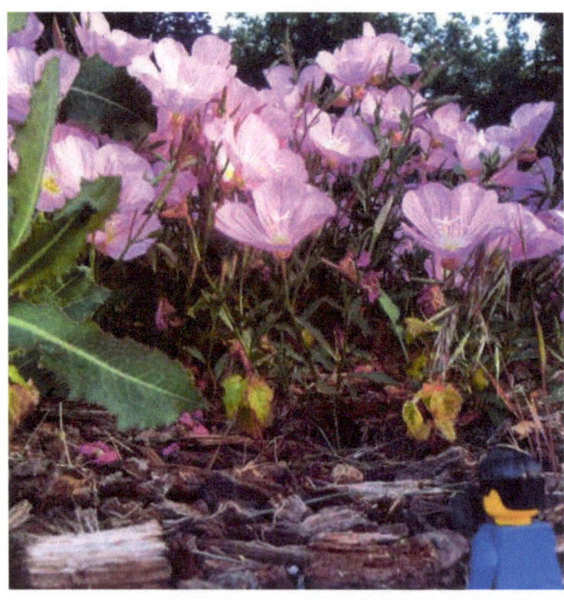
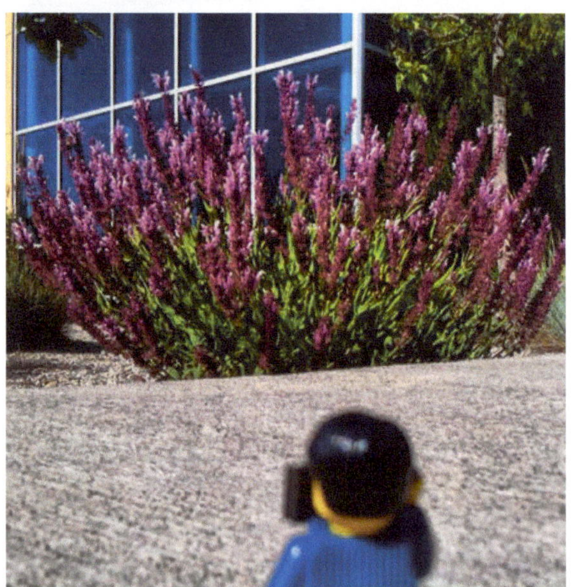

# FOOD, FRUIT, AND FREE HUGS

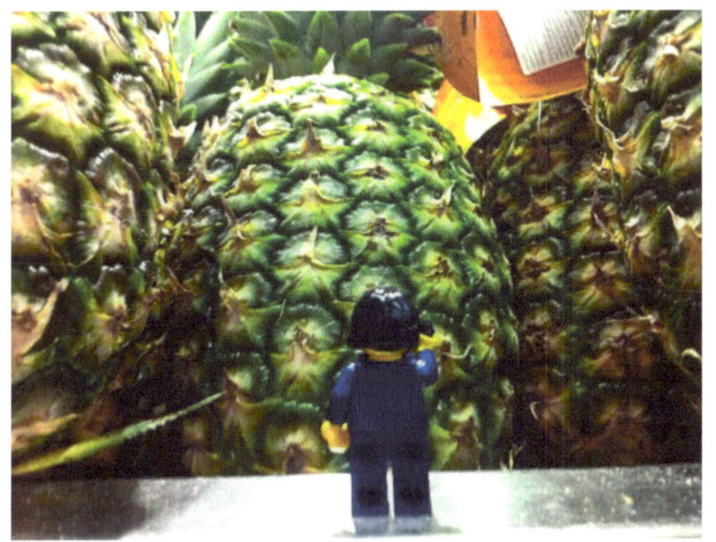

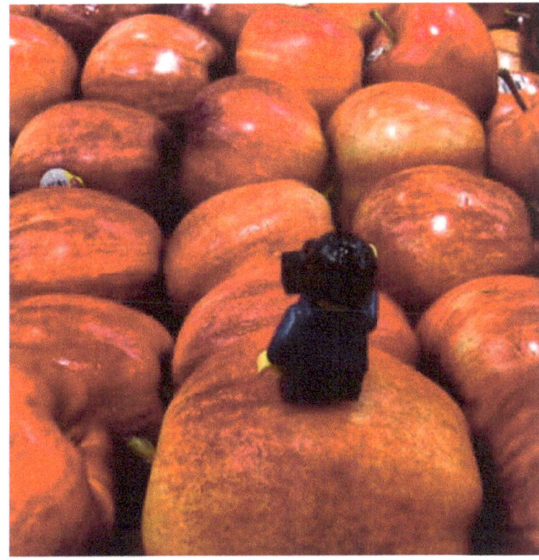

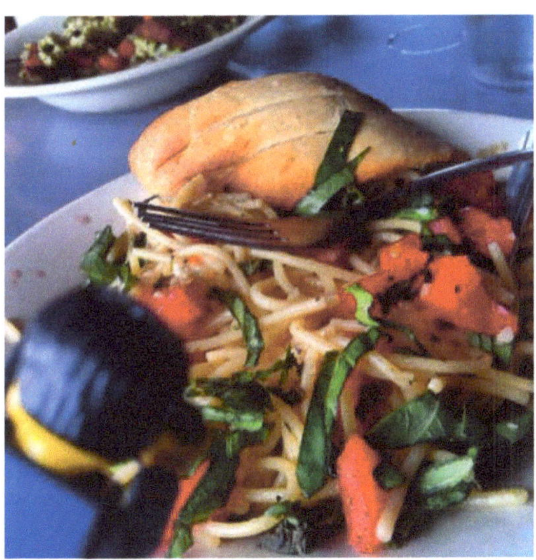

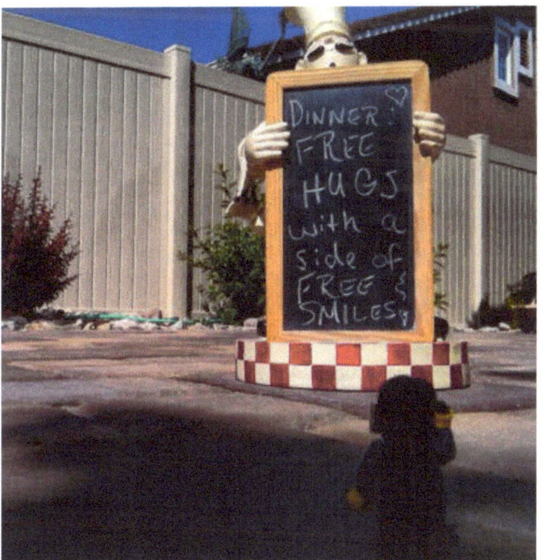


"No one is born a great cook, one learns by doing."     — *Julia Child*

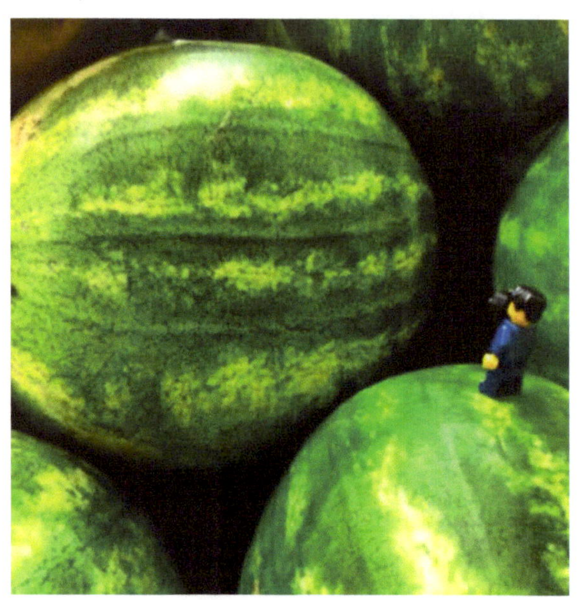

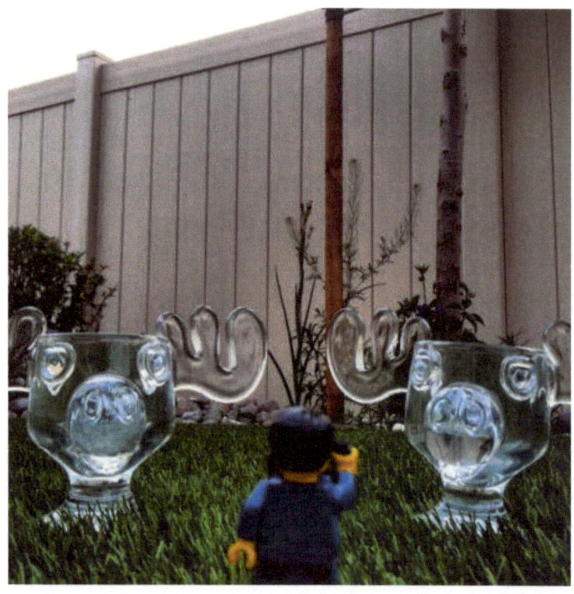

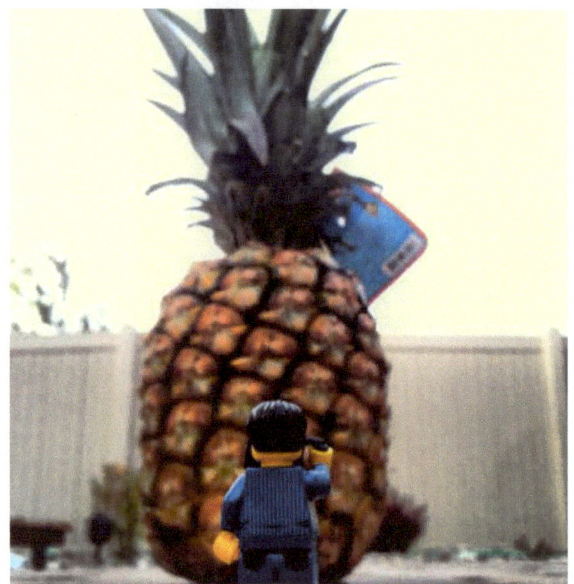

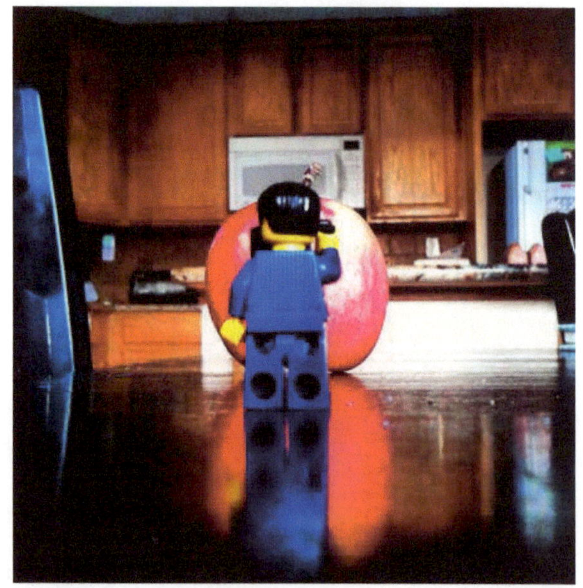

**Team TLC = Thomas, Lillian, Camilla and ... Lovey, the Guinea Pig**

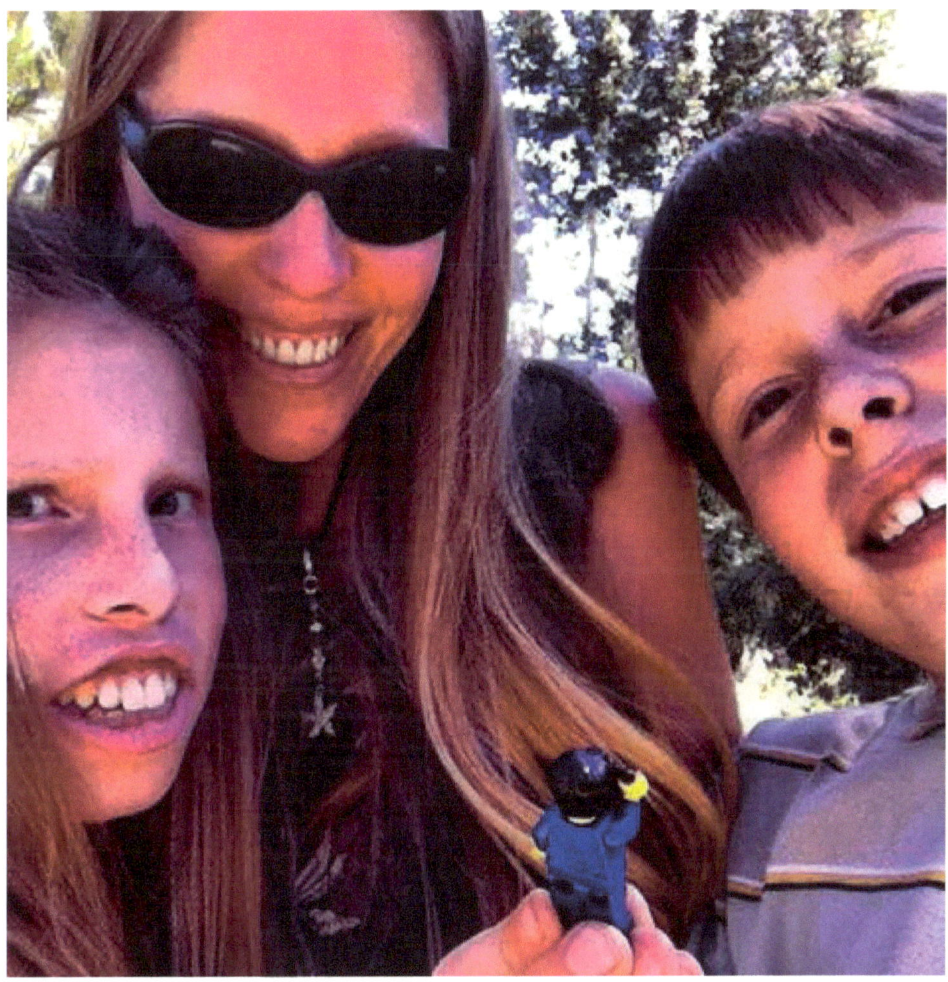

"There are only two ways to live your life. One is as though nothing is a miracle. The other is as though everything is a miracle."
— *Albert Einstein*

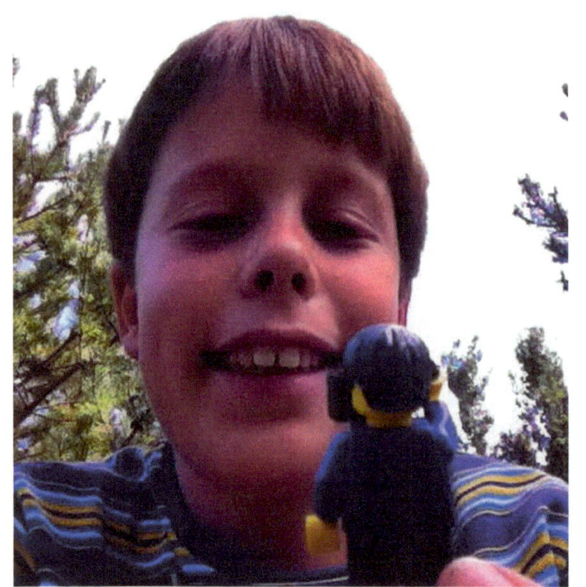
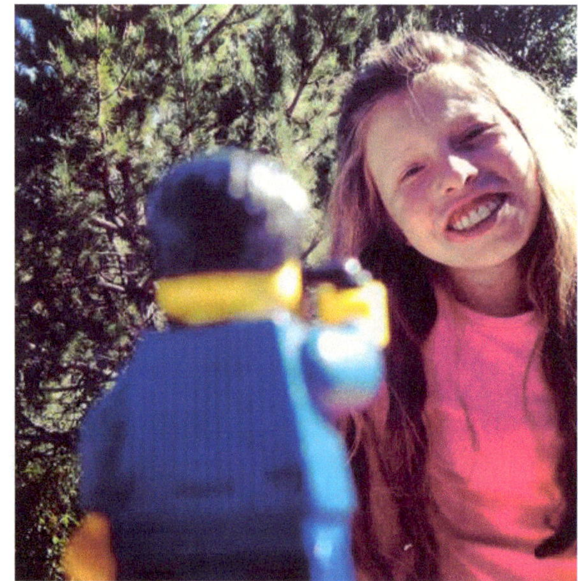
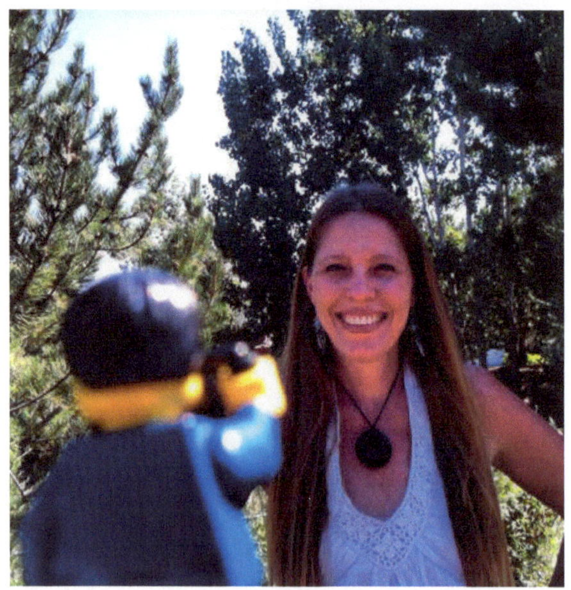
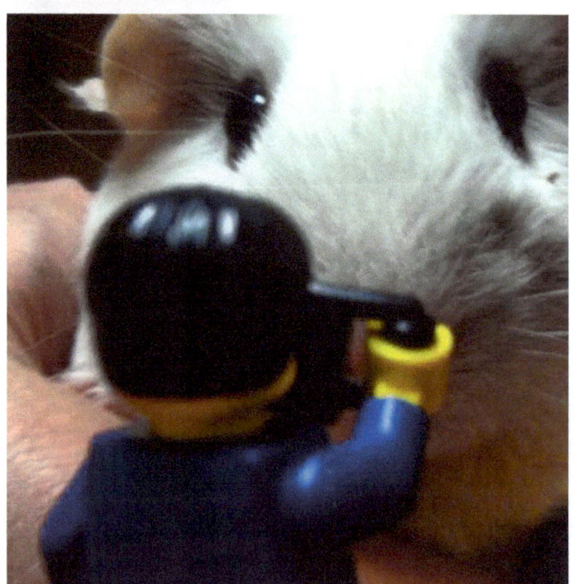

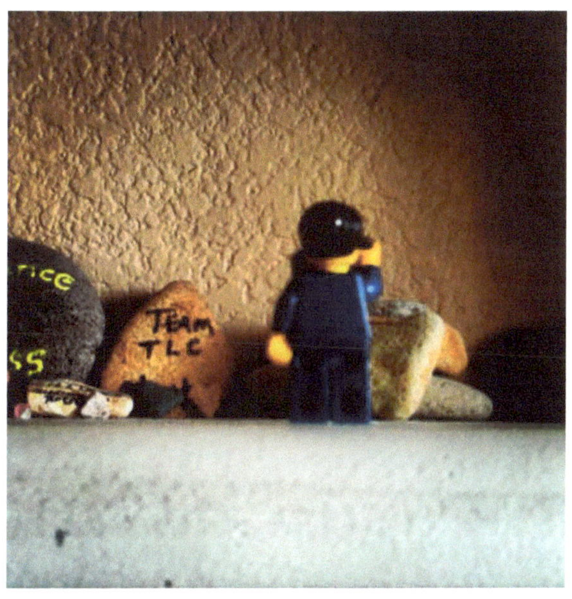

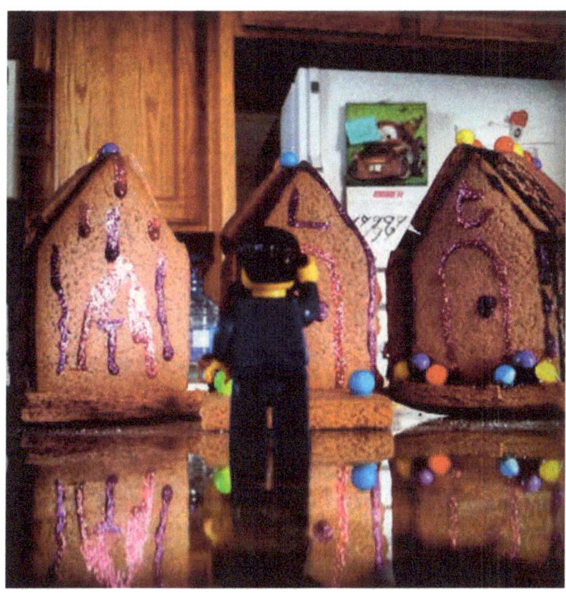

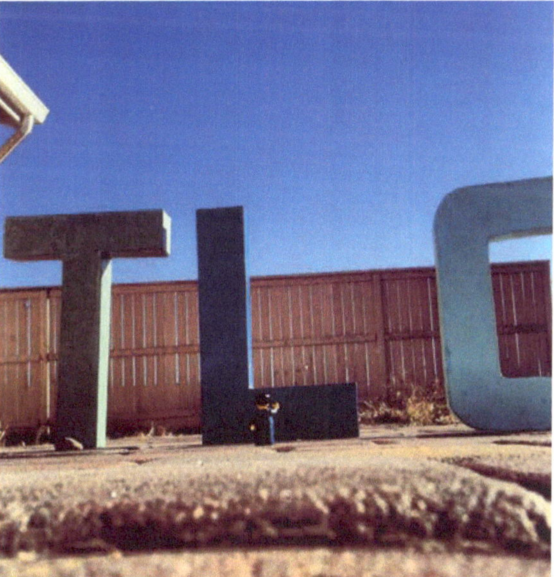

# TEAM TLC MOVIE NIGHT

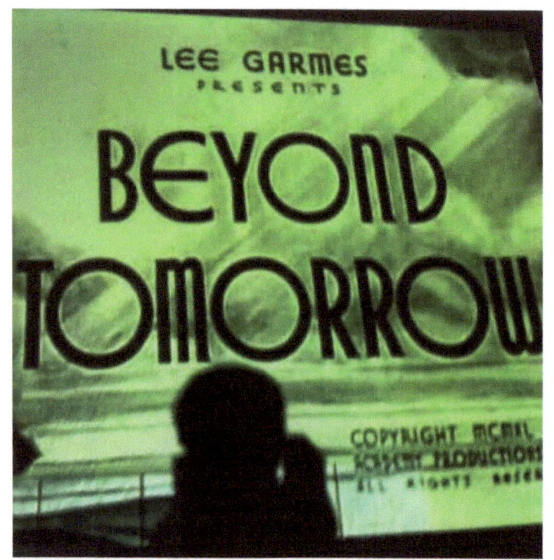


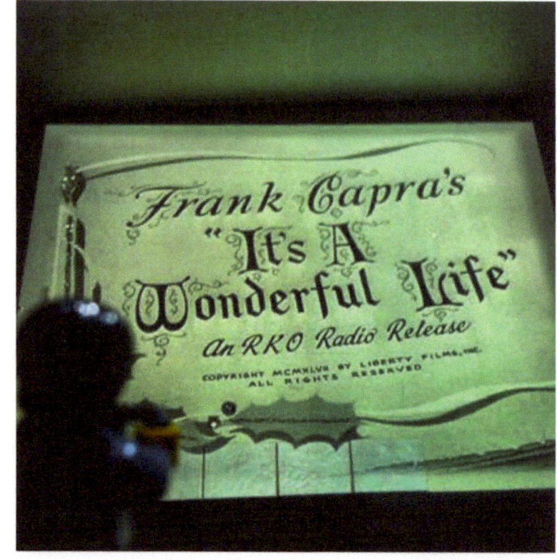


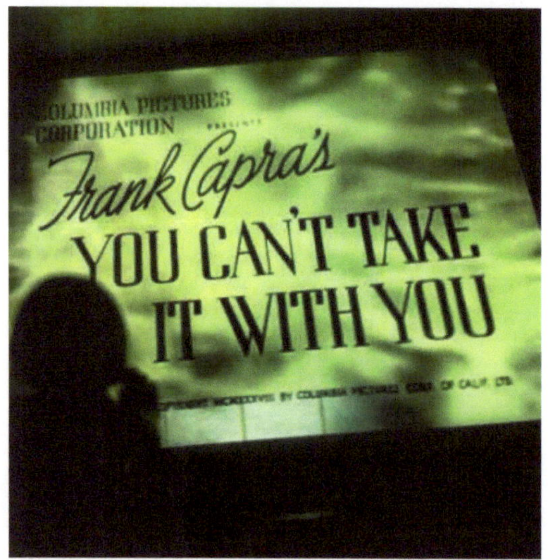


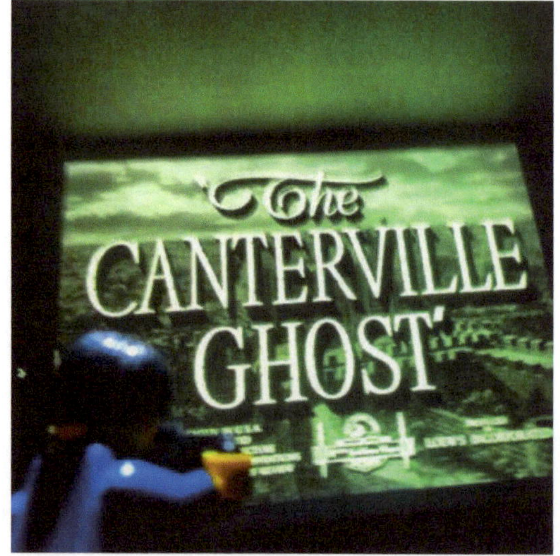


"Everything you can imagine is real."          — Pablo Picasso

# ROCKS, STONES, AND SHELLS!

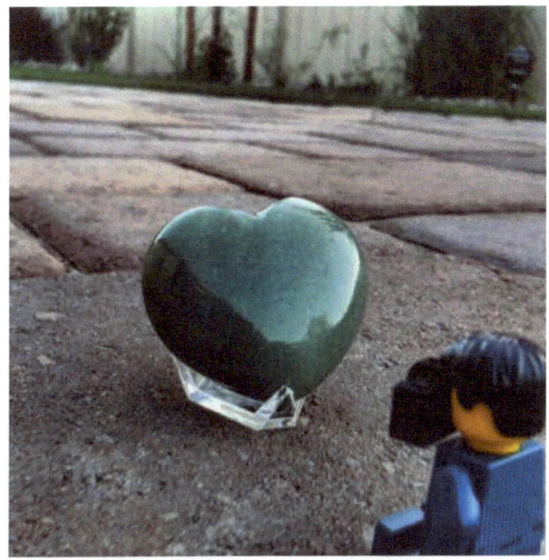

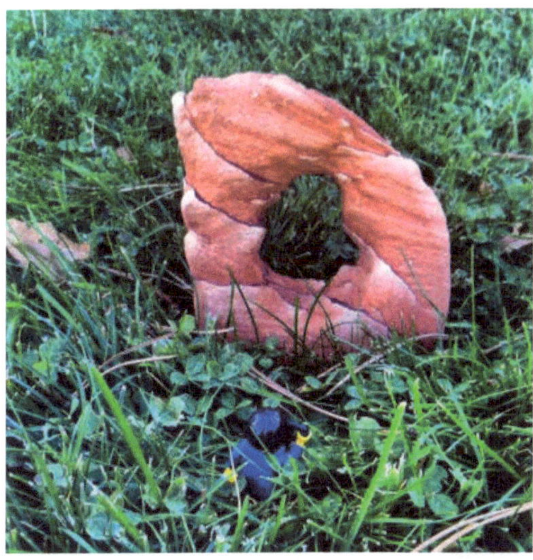

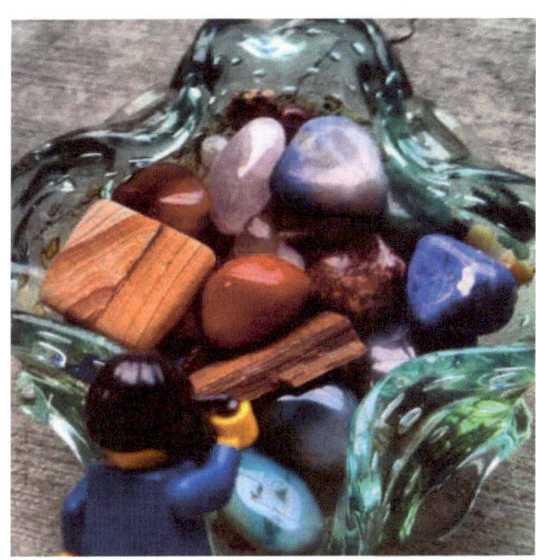

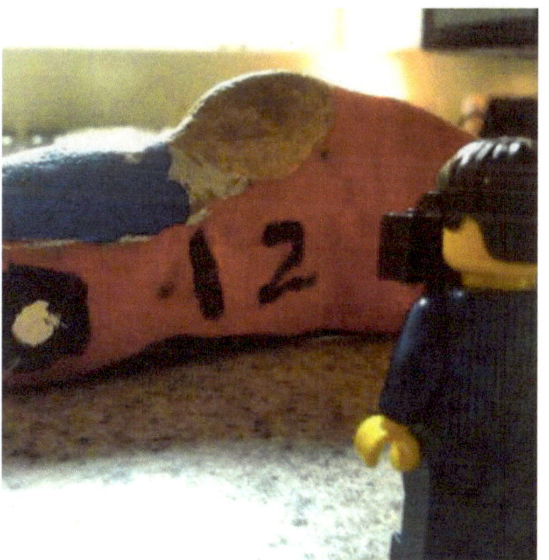

"In every walk with nature, one receives far more than he seeks."
-John Muir

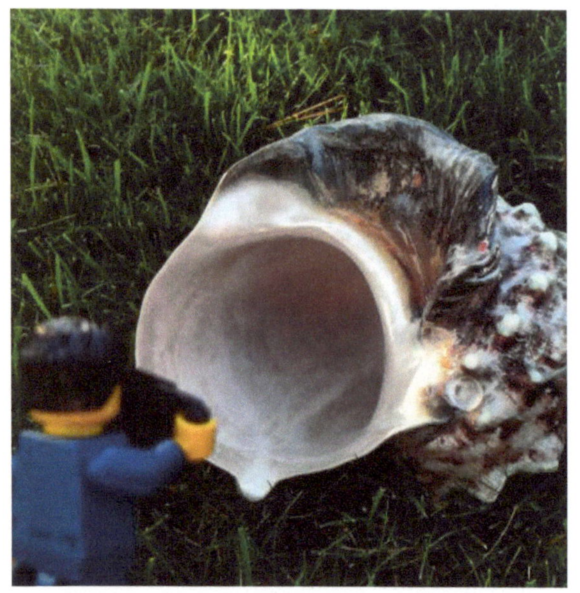
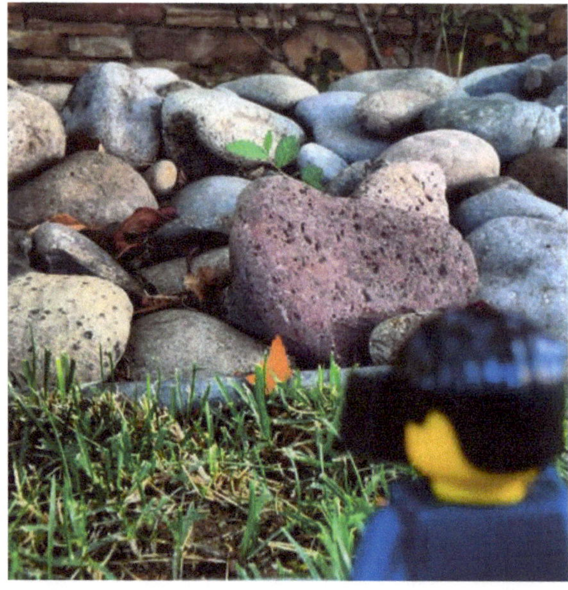
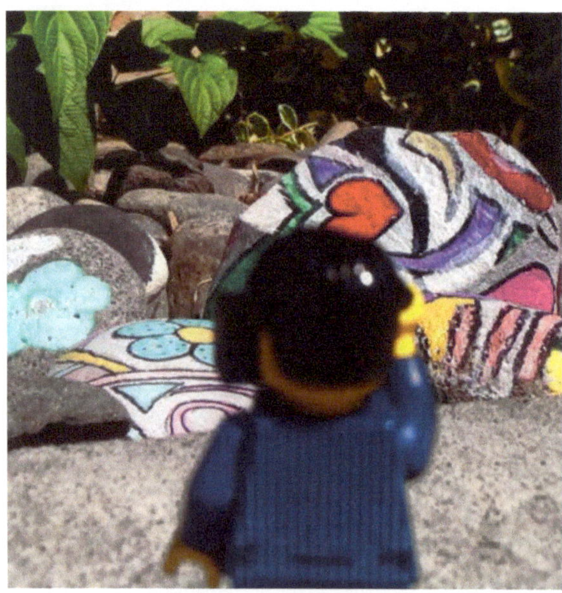
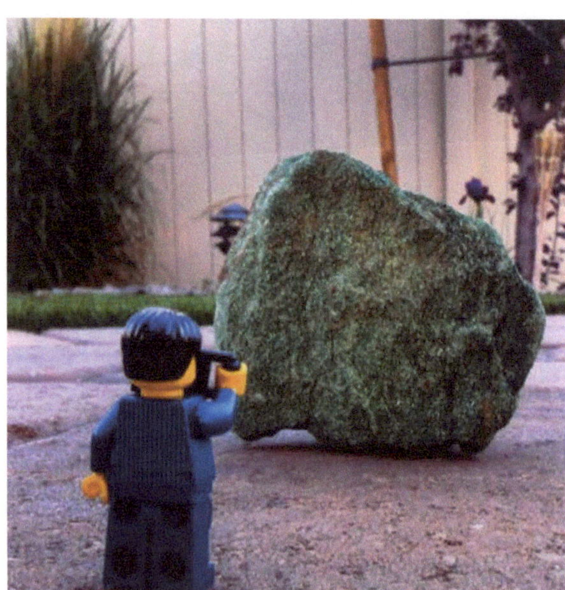

# WE DID IT!!!

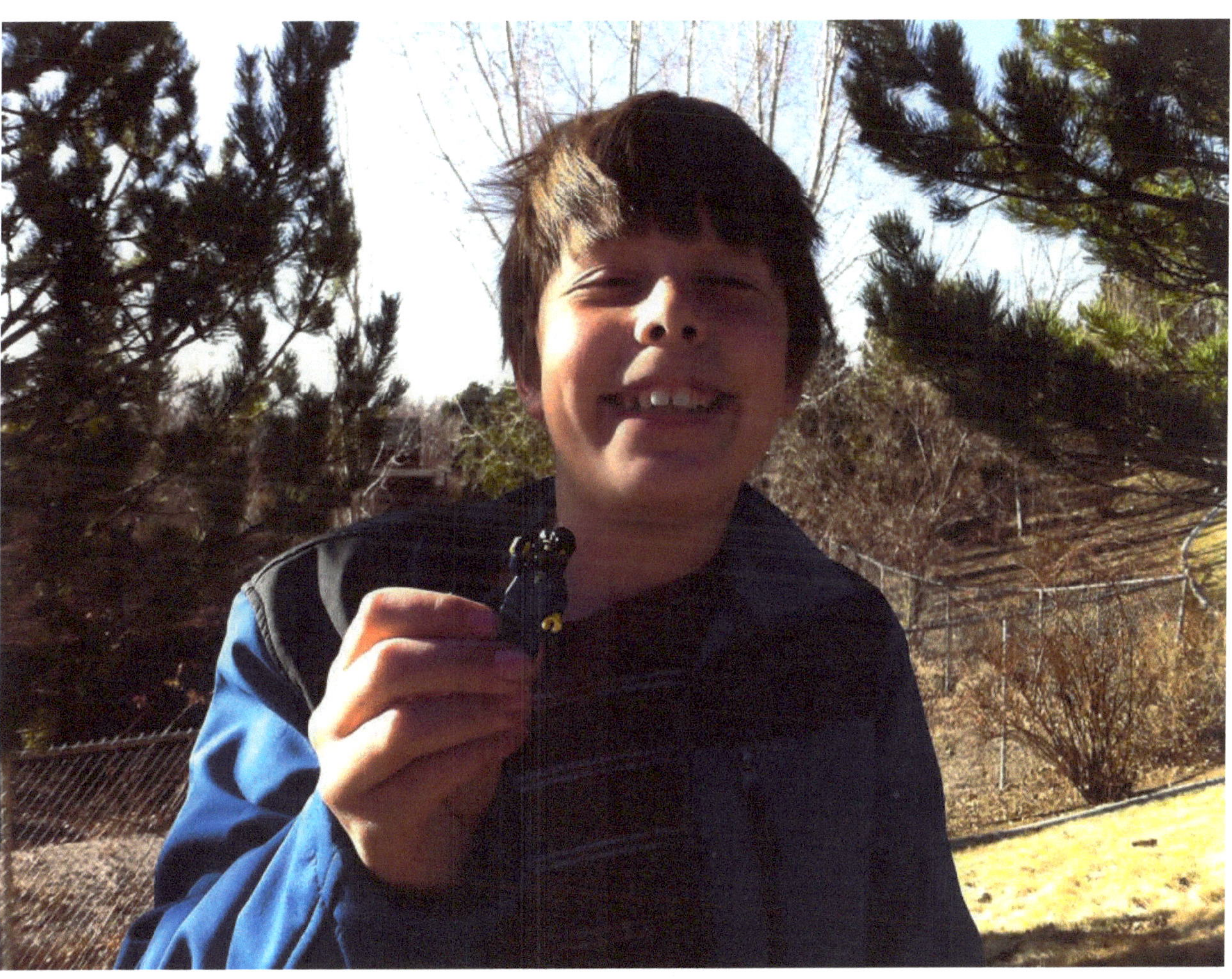

Thomas here. I'd like to leave you with some of my favorite quotes:

"You may say I'm a dreamer, but I'm not the only one. I hope someday you'll join us. And the world will live as one."

— *John Lennon*

"Those who don't believe in magic will never find it."

— *Roald Dahl*

"Anyone who has never made a mistake has never tried anything new."

— *Albert Einstein*

"I have not failed. I've just found 10,000 ways that won't work."

— *Thomas A. Edison*

"Be who you are and say what you feel, because those who mind don't matter, and those who matter don't mind."

— *Bernard M. Baruch*

"Listen to the mustn'ts. Listen to the don'ts. Listen to the shouldn'ts, the impossibles, the won'ts. Listen to the never haves, then listen close to me... Anything can happen. Anything can be."

— *Shel Silverstein*

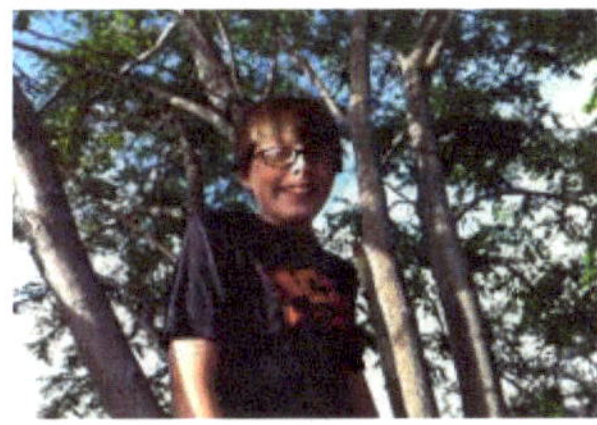

Thomas is now 10 years old and soon to be 11 years old in November 2016. He is homeschooled and some of his favorite topics are minecraft, LEGOS, coding, math, and learning about topics that interest him. He loves fibonacci numbers, bernoulli's equation, and the law of infinite probability. Some of his most cherished things to do are reading, being outside, going on adventures, and swimming. He has a sister, Lillian Darnell, who is also a writer. You can follow Thomas' adventures here:

ThomasADarnell.com  
twitter.com/ThomasDarnell  
instagram.com/ThomasADarnell

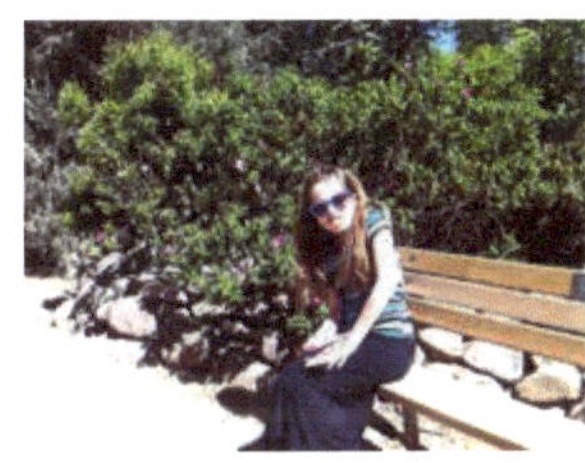

Lillian loves to write fictional stories and loves tracking the weather. She is 15 years old and has a chromosome difference simply called 18p- as it only affects 1 in 50,000 people. You can learn more about Lillian here:

LillianDarnell.com  
instagram.com/LillianDarnell

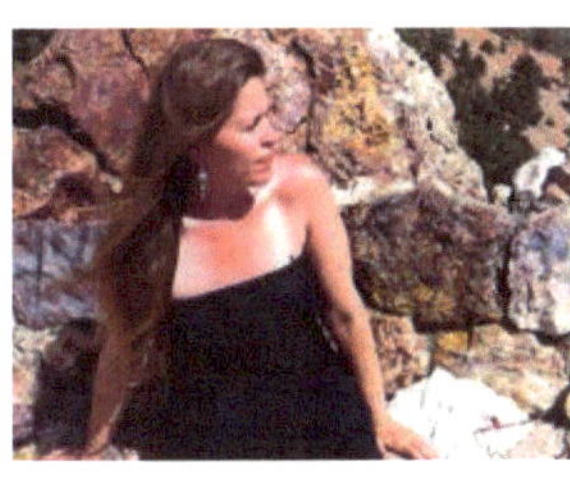

Camilla is Thomas' mom and she is excited for him that this book has finally come to be. She is a mom, best selling author, writer, blogger, and amateur nature photographer. Some of her favorite topics and practices are meditating, mindfulness, and emotional connection. Camilla loves being with her two kids, creating adventures, going for walks, connecting with nature and sharing that with others. You can follow Camilla's adventures at her website, blog and social media outlets at:

CamillaDowns.com  
twitter.com/CamillaDowns  
facebook.com/CamillaDowns  
pinterest.com/CamillaDowns  
instagram.com/CamillaDowns

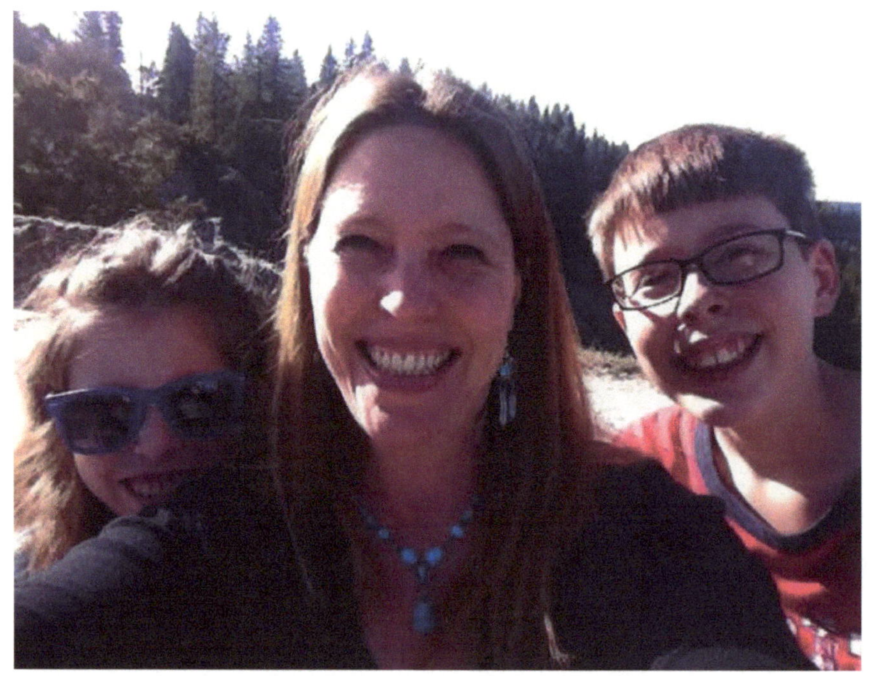

You can follow Team TLC adventures on
our website and blog at:
TheTeamTLC.com

If you enjoyed this book, please share it
with a friend. The website for the book is:
BiggestLittlePhotographer.com.

The book can be purchased on the website
or Amazon. Stay tuned for the ebook
which will include all of the photographs.

**Loving Kindness Books**
a division of
Loving Kindness Publishing
PO Box 19812, Reno, NV 89511
LovingKindnessBooks.com

www.ingramcontent.com/pod-product-compliance
Lightning Source LLC
Chambersburg PA
CBHW042113030726
47599CB00002B/200